A Watered Garden

Christian Worship and Earth's Ecology

Benjamin M. Stewart

AUGSBURG FORTRESS

A WATERED GARDEN
Christian Worship and Earth's Ecology

Editor: Suzanne Burke
Cover design: Laurie Ingram, Tory Herman
Interior design: Laurie Ingram
Cover photo: Fireweed and the Kenai River in Alaska, © Michael Braun/
iStockphoto.com

ISBN 978–0–8066–5393–8

Manufactured in the U.S.A.

17   16   15   14   13   12   11   1   2   3   4   5   6   7

Contents

Preface

Humans seem to have practiced *worship* for as long as we can peer
back into history. Christians, relative newcomers to human history,
have been gathering for worship for nearly 2,000 years. The word *ecology*,
however, is less than 150 years old. And only in recent decades has
the concept of ecology attracted wide interest in dominant Western
cultures. In these recent decades, ecological discoveries have evoked
awe and wonder at the flourishing intricacies of life on earth, and also
horror and denial at the ecological disintegration caused by humanity's
patterns of consumption, disruption, and waste.

Many Christians today are increasingly aware of the earth and its
creatures as gifts from God that are to be loved, cherished, and protected
from degradation or destruction. However, many Western ecological
concepts are relatively new, having emerged long after our Christian
scriptures and liturgical patterns developed. Therefore, ecological concern
can seem like a fad, an awkward import into the Christian faith.
Links between faith and ecology can seem shallow or contrived. Given
the seriousness of our planetary ecological emergency, we will need to
draw on our very deepest liturgical and theological sources for wisdom,
hope, and courage in this long-haul project of ecological healing.

This book begins with the classic, ecumenically-held patterns of
Christian worship and explores them for their deep connections to

ecological wisdom, their sacramental approaches to creation, and for a renewed relationship to the earth now itself in need of God's healing. This book is written especially for North Americans: people who live in a specific ecological region and who play a particular role in the world's ecology. And of course it is written for Christians, especially those who are part of the Lutheran movement. This book is written in the hope that by the power of God the Christian worshiping community and the whole wounded earth may come to flourish with renewed and abundant life. One such promise may resound in our places of worship each year on Ash Wednesday, when we are newly reminded of our mortality, shown the ruins caused by our destructive sin, and told to remember, in words and with ashes, our often-forgotten basic identity as creatures made of dust, of the earth:

> The LORD will guide you continually,
>   and satisfy your needs in parched places,
>   and make your bones strong;
> and you shall be like a watered garden,
>   like a spring of water,
>   whose waters never fail.
> Your ancient ruins shall be rebuilt;
>   you shall raise up the foundations of many generations;
> you shall be called the repairer of the breach,
>   the restorer of streets to live in.
> (Isa. 58:11-12; Ash Wednesday, years A, B, C)

Every book depends on a wider ecology of wisdom, assistance, and inspiration. I am deeply grateful for the many teachers and colleagues who have been important conversation partners with me in the subjects of this book, some of whom include Joyce Flueckiger, Gordon Lathrop, Joy McDougal, and Don Saliers; Susan Briehl, Marty Haugen, Mary Preus, and Tom Witt; and gifted editor Suzanne Burke at Augsburg Fortress. And a few living places, too, have especially shaped my sense of the earth's ecology with which Christian worship is here in dialog: Copper Basin and the Railroad Creek Valley; Illinois' Salt Creek between Fullersberg Woods and the Des Plaines River; and Glacier National Park, especially its great cascades and glaciers, and the hope held by its people, land, and diverse creatures that they may one day return to their flourishing glory. Most profound thanks go to the little band of fellow worshipers and earth-lovers with whom I most regularly and joyfully share the treasures of earth and Christian worship: Forrest and Justin, and especially Beth.

1
Worship and Ecology

Worship and ecology: an odd couple?

The topics of ecology and Christian worship aren't often considered together, so a book that combines them into a single theme might be a curiosity for you. Perhaps you are excited to see these two important subjects explored together in a single book. Such a combination might also raise suspicions. Is the book actually using Christian worship to advance a narrow political viewpoint? Or is it intended to make Christian worship simply *seem* more environmentally relevant—to "greenwash" Christian worship? Or perhaps it is an attempt to be trendy or novel; some popular books intentionally create an unlikely pairing for the sake of novelty, or even as a joke: *The Simpsons and Philosophy*, or *Flower Arranging for Stock Brokers*, for example. This little book begins with the conviction that Christian worship and ecology are not novelties or small topics. They are both deep and broad, and are matters of life and death.

Take the English word *worship*. It is derived from the Middle English word *worth-ship*, which refers to the act of ascribing worth, or value, to something. So someone putting prices on items at an estate sale is engaged in an act of worth-ship. Everything in the estate is assigned a measure of worth: a box of buttons, a set of crystal goblets, a rusty bucket, a handmade mahogany desk. The worth of everything in the environment of the estate is considered and measured.

Unlike an estate sale, Christian worship doesn't ascribe monetary worth to things. Christian worship is, however, an act of worth-ship in which Christians ascribe ultimate worth to God and in which we may find everything in our own environment ascribed surprising measures of worth by the living Word of God. The book of Proverbs values wisdom as "better than gold, even fine gold" (Prov. 8:19). Jesus underscores the worth of God and neighbor, saying, "Love the Lord your God with all your heart, and with all your soul, and with all your strength, and with all your mind; and your neighbor as yourself" (Luke 10:27). The worth of God's people can be measured in apparently paradoxical ways: you are dust, and to dust you shall return (Gen. 3:19), and yet, you are a chosen race, a royal priesthood, a holy nation, God's own people (1 Peter 2:9). At baptism, declarations of the newly baptized's worth are abundant: "Child of God, you have been sealed by the Holy Spirit and marked with the cross of Christ forever" (*Evangelical Lutheran Worship*, 231). At a funeral, the dead are ascribed worth in God, as the presider commends to God "a sheep of your own fold, a lamb of your own flock, a sinner of your own redeeming" (*Evangelical Lutheran Worship*, 283). And, over literally *everything* in the cosmos, God's own original ascription of worth still resounds in our liturgies: God saw everything that had been made, and indeed, it was very good (Gen. 1:31).

So, Christian worship is, among other things, *worth-ship*. It is an act that ascribes worth to God, to us, and to the whole environment around us, stretching out to include the entire "very good" cosmos. In short, the horizon of concern in Christian worship extends outward to the entire universe.

Next, consider the concept of ecology. Ecology, by definition, has to do with the interdependence of . . . *everything*. Asking ecological questions often means focusing on or beginning with living things on

Earth, yet it inevitably involves even realities far outside of Earth: the moon's gravity lifts Earth's large bodies of water toward the moon's surface, forming Earth's tides; most of the energy in our food has recently traveled 93 million miles across space at light speed from our nearest star, the sun, and is stored on Earth by green plants; more than two tons of natural materials from outer space fall to the earth every day, becoming part of our soil, water, food, and bodies. And the bulk of the earth itself is made of materials formed out of the explosions of ancient stars. So ecology, too, extends outward toward the mysterious horizons of the universe.

But ecology also moves toward closer horizons, equally mysterious. Your own hands that hold the book you are now reading are themselves made of earth—made of water that has fallen many times as rain, salts from the oceans, minerals from the farms' fields, perhaps energy that had been stored in the milk or flesh of other animals. The book itself—and every other manufactured thing in the space around you—is made exclusively of materials that have either been grown from the earth or mined out of it. Ecology stretches out to the boundaries of the universe yet also reaches deep within us, into each of our cells.

Thus ecology and Christian worship both extend outward toward "everything," to attend to the worth of things, their interconnections with things seen and unseen, and their place in the whole living creation. Their consideration together in a single theme is no novelty, but rather a natural partnership. Both are, in fact, ways of seeing everything as part of the one great whole. Nothing is considered irrelevant or outside of their scope of vision. Both attend to the very small and close at hand (grains of sand, a mustard seed) and extend outward to the widest horizons, beyond our knowing (the foundations of the earth, the depths of the sea, the stars of the heavens, all that is, seen and unseen).

Many present-day cultures do indeed find the pairing of ecology and Christian worship to be odd. That may be a symptom of just how shrunken our cultures' visions of both worship and ecology have become; they are considered niche topics. It is hoped that this book can deepen appreciation for the wonders of both ecology and Christian worship, even while finding the partnership between these two expansive ways of knowing as natural, true, and even necessary.

New questions for an ancient faith: discoveries of the ecological era

While Christian worship and ecology are indeed natural partners, and have been so since the beginning of Christianity, the current era has seen a number of discoveries—perhaps so significant as to be called revelations—that pose pressing questions for both Christian worship and ecology. In the last few centuries, and coming to a climax at the turn of the twenty-first century, Earth's human societies have discovered many fundamental realities that most societies did not (and largely *could* not) know until now. It is helpful to review some of these discoveries that are particularly relevant to Christian worship.

What's up with heaven?

Over the past centuries, using mathematical calculations, telescopes, and now satellites and space probes, humanity has discovered and come to wide agreement that *up* is not *heaven* or *the heavens* but is mostly empty space, of which Earth is not the center. This agreement poses questions about how we interpret some of our ancient liturgical language, for example, the liturgical confession that Jesus "came down from heaven" in the Nicene Creed. While Earth is not the center of the universe, or of the Milky Way, or even of our little solar system, given everything we can see or detect, Earth is *unique*. While we may someday discover life outside of Earth, nearly every other place we have looked in the universe appears to be violently inhospitable to life. For example, our moon is around 238,000 miles from Earth. Many people have traveled so many miles in recent times. Some frequent flier program minimums start at 100,000 miles. So why don't frequent fliers visit the moon ("the heavens") instead of Hawaii or Cleveland or Paris? The answer is simple: because all of the territory we know outside of Earth's thin atmosphere is profoundly hostile to life. We didn't know that until recently. But the pre-space-travel idea of heaven being an inhabitable place up above us is deeply rooted in our scriptural and liturgical traditions. So how shall we receive, interpret, and pass on these traditions to our children and other new Christians in this space-age era? How shall we deal with liturgical images in scripture, hymns, and prayers that locate God or heaven "up" above us?[1]

Shaking the foundations: rediscovering the earth

Our image of the heavens is not the only image to shift radically within relatively recent history. Our primary image of the *earth* has changed over the past few centuries as well. It went from being the ground floor, the foundation, of everything that is, with only a dome of the heavens above, and perhaps a mysterious underworld below, to something much less universally central. In 1968, the photo *Earthrise* pictured the earth as a small object above the barren face of the moon, and in 1972 the photo of the full view of Earth from space became the most reproduced image in human history. For the first time, Earth was photographed as a small, manipulable object in a much larger field. One astronaut reported alarm at seeing what he had thought of as "an ocean of air"—Earth's atmosphere—appearing from space to be only a slight film over its surface. In fact, the depth of Earth's atmosphere—what we experience as that "ocean of air" into which all our tailpipes and smokestacks empty—is best measured by looking at a classroom desktop globe: the layer of atmosphere surrounding Earth is as thin, proportionally, as the layer of varnish covering the globe.

When humans saw Earth and its atmosphere from space, it only deepened the shock we felt when we found that Earth wasn't the center of the universe. The milestone marked by the first photo of

Earth taken from space occurred within the lifetimes of many of our present-day church members. As a human community, we are still in the midst of the same radical shifts in our knowledge and perspective as those associated with Galileo's telescope. The ancient view of Earth as the ground floor and foundation of the universe—a view largely assumed by our scriptures and inherited liturgical texts—is being challenged by new ways of seeing. In light of these new visions, how shall we read ancient texts, preach, pray, and sing about God's earth in worship?

Measuring the worth of the "very good" creation

One of the classical Western ways of imaging the order of the universe was what some have called the "Great Chain of Being." At the very top of this hierarchy were beings that were considered both spiritual and male: God, and then angels. Next were those made up of both spirit and flesh: humans, with males higher in the hierarchy and considered more intellectual and spiritual than females. Females, according to the males who passed on this narrative, were associated more with the body and the earth, and were therefore lower. And then downward from humans were the higher animals and then the lower animals, and then plants, dirt, and rock.

One of the strongest and most successful critiques of this hierarchy came from the school of thought generally identified as *feminism*, and thus we might also include feminism in the history of ecological revelations. One oversimplified way of defining feminism is the conviction that voices in addition to those of powerful males matter. Feminism as a broad movement has given voice to ideas that were not officially supposed to exist, let alone be spoken. This has led, quite recently, to the ordination of women in some Christian communities. This movement has overlapped with and helped to strengthen similar movements that attend to other suppressed voices and experiences. Feminism has critiqued the Great Chain of Being by insisting on the equality of men's and women's worth. It has also at times, together with many traditional indigenous worldviews, inspired questions about the entire Great Chain of Being and the disregard shown to creatures considered lower than others. Laws have recently been enacted to protect nonhuman animals and plants from abuse on an individual level and from extinction as species. These laws—together with recent advances toward gender equality—are evidence of profound shifts occurring in the present era around the question of how "worth" is measured. How do these shifts in our ways of attributing worth affect how we shall worship (or *worth-ship*)? How do we intercede differently for other creatures when we approach them with a deeper appreciation for their inherent value?

A new, shared creation story

The prevailing scientific theories of the emergence of the universe and life on Earth have been developed over the past two centuries. Many people and societies still struggle to comprehend and accept them, even as the theories are well established in scientific communities. Theologian Sallie McFague, in her *The Body of God: An Ecological Theology*, calls these theories "the common creation story," because they are globally shared *scientific* narratives of creation that can be held in common by cultures around the world, even while these cultures may continue to honor, cherish, and hand down their own ancient, *religious* creation narratives alongside the scientific stories (Fortress Press, 1993, 38–64). The common creation story, like many religious creation stories, invites us to contemplate a time when there was no life on Earth, no planet Earth at all, and not even a universe as we know it. Such stories may move us toward wonder, gratitude, and even fear given the apparent contingency of our earthly existence.

Perhaps most powerfully, this common creation story can surprise us by the relatively recent emergence of modern humans on earth. Scientists estimate that life emerged on Earth around 4 billion years ago, and that primates developed around 65 million years ago, with modern humans emerging between 100,000 and 200,000 years ago.

These numbers are hard for us to put into perspective, so consider another measure. If the first simple living creatures emerged on Earth one hour ago, then fish have been swimming in the oceans for the equivalent of around eight minutes. Primates emerged just one minute ago, and modern humans only in the last less-than-half-second. By any measure, humans are very recent arrivals to the earth and to its community of living species. How should prayers and sermons speak about the origins of life and of the cosmos, considering the truths of both the common creation story and the scriptural narratives of creation? What sort of humility and wonder is appropriate in our hymns for God's care for Earth's living creatures who long preceded human beings? Do we pray differently now that we know we are such newcomers to the earth?[2]

Engineering and end times

With the twentieth century's two world wars and the first two attacks using atomic weapons, theologian Paul Tillich wrote that, for the first time in human history, "the end" came into view as a matter of historical likelihood. Cultures and religions have often imagined a cosmic end to all things, but the recent critical change for religious traditions is that the threat of a cosmic-scale end to life had been, in previous eras, a threat typically understood as arising from supernatural beings, or from natural, cosmic forces. During the twentieth century the threat became clearly the human species itself. This milestone poses new religious, existential, and ethical questions of awful significance. How shall Christian worship account for this utterly new ecological threat: a humanly engineered catastrophic end to civilization, to the human species, and perhaps even to all life on Earth?

However, even without the use of our most fearsome weapons, human disruption of Earth's ecology has already placed us in the midst of what many scientists describe as the greatest mass extinction since the age of the dinosaurs 65 million years ago. The current ecological emergency is more pressing than any other ecological crisis in human history. And some of the proposed human responses to this emergency are themselves disturbing. Theoretical astrophysicist Stephen Hawking has warned that humans must leave planet Earth in the next century in order to escape the threat of human extinction arising from ecological collapse, calling space colonization "our only chance of long-term survival."[3] Others, in the face of planetary ecological emergencies, have begun calling for various "geo-engineering" strategies (for example, attempting to cool the overheated planet by putting mirrors in orbit around it to reduce the amount of sunlight shining on Earth). Proposals like these from Hawking and from advocates of geo-engineering call on human society not to scale back human manipulation of our ecological environment, but rather to increase radically human control over Earth and over any other environment humans may inhabit. As humanity faces increasingly radical proposals that attempt to manipulate the ecological systems of planet Earth, how shall Christian worship continue to confess that "the earth is the LORD's" (Ps. 24:1) and that with God humans are only "aliens and tenants" of the land (Lev. 25:23)? When some even begin to make plans to leave behind planet Earth as if it were disposable, what resources and practices will help Christians continue to pray for the flourishing of Earth, to sing its goodness, and to honor the One who made it our home?

The earth as a fellow creature

All of these recent ecological and cosmic discoveries can be disorienting, as they are seismic shifts in humanity's worldviews: an Earth not physically at the center of anything other than the moon's orbit and surrounded by largely empty space; increasing appreciation for the inherent worth and dignity of Earth's nonhuman creatures; the astonishingly brief time in which human beings have inhabited the earth compared to the long history of other species; the threat of a sudden catastrophic end to human civilization at the hands of human weaponry; and the increasingly desperate ecological emergencies (and strategies for survival) facing humanity. In the end, as disorienting as these shifts are, the upshot of all of them is relatively straightforward. Rather than knowing the earth as the ecologically unchanging "ground floor" of the entire cosmos (one-half of the universe), we are now coming to know the earth as it actually is. The earth is a relatively small living creature, in many ways like us: fragile, created good, in need of healing, part of a living community, alive, and mortal.

A place in creation's choir

The prayer of thanksgiving at the table during Easter proclaims that our human gathering for worship joins in the "unending hymn" already being sung by "earth and sea and all their creatures." The psalms we sing in worship attest that the sky proclaims its maker's handiwork (Ps. 19:1), that everything that has breath praises the Lord (Ps. 150:6), and that a glorious global choir of water, sun, moon, stars, fire, hail, snow, fog, wind, mountains, hills, trees, land animals, fish, and birds joins in a song of praise to God (Ps. 148:4-10). Christian worship has always been an act of joining the wider worship of the whole creation, a liturgy that began long before humans even existed. In this era, through a variety of means, Christians and others have come to hear more deeply the hymns of praise, the songs of lament, and, yes, even the prophetic accusations of guilt that the creation is singing and even groaning all around and within us.

In this present era, the human relationship with the earth has changed more rapidly than at any other time in human history. We have damaged and threatened God's Earth more perilously and completely than any species before us, and yet, in this very same era, we have come to know more about the wonders of God's Earth and its ecology, and about our dependent place in it, than ever before. Our knowledge seems to be opening a path, as we may sing, to "life's destruction or our most triumphant hour" ("God, who stretched the spangled heavens," ELW 771). In a church that is always reforming, how will our worship life (our hymns, our prayers, our rituals, our worship spaces, our preaching) be reformed in light of these most profound advances in knowledge about our home planet and our place in it? By taking part in this conversation you are already part of how the church is responding to unprecedented discoveries about the vital interdependencies of God's wondrous creation.

How this book is organized

The organization of this book's chapters brings attention to the physical, earthy nature of our worship. Christian worship does not just happen in the abstract or appear out of thin air. As Gordon Lathrop puts it with refreshing simplicity in his book *Holy Things: A Liturgical Theology*, in order to gather faithfully for our chief Sunday service, "we do need some things," including the book of scripture, bread and wine and vessels for sharing, often water, and a gathering of humans (Fortress Press, 2003, 89). So the chapters in this book highlight the place of water in baptism, Earth's relationship to sun and moon in our seasons and days, fields and vineyards in holy communion, and the very earth of our bodies. These are some of the most obvious ways in which Christian worship has earthly rootedness. Notice, then, that the organization of this book embodies a confidence and conviction that the classic places of encounter with the Christian God in worship, animated by the living Word of God, are also places that can take us deeply into ecological truth, healing, and promise. They are, in the language of scripture, "holy ground" (Exod. 3:5).

Finally, something of a caveat: worship and ecology both, as noted above, relate to *everything*. And this is a small book. The chapters in this book are more like short hikes into an expansive ecosystem than they are like definitive and detailed maps or travel guides for an entire area. So here are two assumptions about the way this book will be used. First, these explorations—short hikes—are a tiny part of our long-haul journey of coming to terms with our ecological emergency and identity. All of humanity is now on this journey, including every Christian congregation. So this little book offers only a glimpse into how congregations will continue to think and pray about the reform of Christian worship in this age of ecological emergency and renewal. Second, this book assumes appreciation for and immersion in ecumenical liturgical practice, especially as embodied in *Evangelical Lutheran Worship* and its family of resources. The practices embodied in these resources are a beginning point for the explorations in this small book, and their wise counsel and life-giving patterns of prayer of course can only be inadequately covered here. Thus, there are two other conversation partners assumed in the reading of this book: participation in the long-haul journey toward ecological renewal of the earth (including implications on the congregational level), as well as deep engagement with ongoing liturgical renewal, especially as embodied in *Evangelical Lutheran Worship* and its family of resources.

For reflection and discussion

1. Recall a time in Sunday worship in which you sensed God's presence filling all things. Describe your experience. Have you had such an experience outdoors, in a natural setting? If so, how are these two experiences related in your own faith?
2. Do you struggle with the ecological and scientific discoveries described in this chapter? Do friends or family struggle with them?
3. What images of ecological catastrophe have you encountered in the news or in popular entertainment? Perhaps you have read Cormac McCarthy's novel *The Road* or seen the Disney/Pixar movie *Wall-E* or the documentary *An Inconvenient Truth*. How is the future imagined in popular culture?
4. Should some Christian liturgical language be adjusted in light of recent scientific discoveries about the earth, its creatures, and its place in the universe? If so, how?

5. The photo *Earthrise* was taken on Christmas day by the Apollo 8 astronauts as they returned from the far side of the moon. Watch the short video clip, "Earthrise, Then and Now," assembled by the *New York Times'* Andrew Revkin, on the fortieth anniversary of *Earthrise*, at http://dotearth.blogs.nytimes.com/2008/12/24/happy-birthday -earthrise/. How do you respond to this image of the earth as a smaller, distant object in space?

2
Water

Praying at the water

For as long as humans have prayed, they have probably prayed at water-places. Water, in so many of its forms and environments, often moves us to wonder, joy, terror, or peace, and many times, in all these things, to prayer: the awesome power of ocean waves; the cold upwelling waters of a spring; a small, still pond; the sound of a mountain stream flowing over rocks; deep, slow rivers with creatures rippling the surface; crashing waterfalls; nourishing rain on parched land as well as overwhelming floods destroying crops and homes; the seemingly infinite expanse of the sea; even hot springs rising mysteriously from the earth. Water often calls us to wonder and prayer.

The Christian heritage of praying next to water is older than Christianity itself, being deeply influenced by our Jewish heritage. One of our stunning water-prayer treasures is Psalm 104. In it, the psalmist looks out over a water-nourished landscape, teeming with abundant creatures and life, and gives thanks to God for blessings that overflow from God to humans and to the whole earth like water streaming down:

You, O God, lay the beams of your chambers in the waters above;
you make the clouds your chariot;
you ride on the wings of the wind.
You make springs gush forth in the valleys;
they flow between the hills,
giving drink to every wild animal;
the wild donkeys quench their thirst.
By the streams the birds of the air have their home;
they sing among the branches.
From your lofty home you water the mountains;
the earth is satisfied with the fruitfulness of your creation.
You make the grass to grow for the cattle,
and plants for people to use,
to bring forth food from the earth,
and wine to gladden the human heart,
oil to make the face shine,
and bread to strengthen the human heart.
The trees of the Living God are watered abundantly,
the cedars of Lebanon that you planted.
In them the birds build their nests;
the stork has its home in the fir trees.
O Living One, how diverse are your creatures!
In wisdom you have made them all;
the earth is full of your creatures.[1]

One might ask after reading this psalm: What is flowing down from the mountains and the skies with such powerful blessings? What is it that is giving life to the diverse creatures named in the psalm? Is it water? Is it God? The beautiful answer is, of course, *both*, simultaneously.

Something important is happening in psalms like this one—something that doesn't always happen in our prayers. A comparison may be helpful. When we sing Psalm 23, *the Lord is my shepherd,* in worship, we give thanks that God acts like a good shepherd. And while we may also be grateful to God for real-life shepherds and real-life woolly sheep, Psalm 23 is not really about agricultural laborers or livestock. Psalm 104, on the other hand, is indeed about giving thanks that God *acts like* nourishing water flowing through our world; however, it is also about giving thanks to God *for the actual water* that flowed thousands of years ago over the psalmist's local landscape, and, perhaps even more, it is about giving thanks for the water that flows around us today, nourishing our lands and all creatures, as we pray this psalm.

Many of us have known scenes such as the one in Psalm 104, and have been ourselves moved to prayers of gratitude: a great panorama of life, in which diverse creatures flourish and the land produces bountifully, all of it watered by nourishing rain and flowing streams. Psalm 104 offers a way of praying beside water in which our prayer does not leave the water behind as a disposable symbol. Rather the prayer beside the water calls forth our sustained attention to the ecological marvels of water—in order to appreciate the very real physical blessings that water provides to the earth, and also because we find deep and scripturally resonant images of the overflowing blessings of God in water flowing over the landscape.

The water beside which the psalmist prayed, however, was not a single, simple location. The psalmist contemplated, at least in the mind's eye, an *entire watershed*—from the heavens' rains and the mountain springs, down through streams flowing between the hills, into fertile valleys and out into the sea. How might a vision as grand as Psalm 104 be glimpsed at our local baptisms and in our worship spaces?

Baptism into Christ has always been an entrance into water (just as our death in Christ, the completion of our baptism, will be an entrance into the earth, the depths, where we are held both in Christ and in the earth). And while baptismal theology has much to say about ecological ethics and eco-theology, this chapter is mostly about the actual rite of baptism itself and the direct connections to ecological realities that arise in the watery enactment of baptism. First, let us consider the *place* of baptism.

Come to the water: places for baptism

In what sort of water do we baptize? How does the water-place look, feel, and sound? What sort of prayer does the place evoke?

The Gospels introduce baptism as occurring on the edge of wilderness. People went out from populated places to the wild locale of John the Baptist, who presided over baptisms in the Jordan River, with John's own voice crying out in the wilderness over the water. Jesus himself was baptized there, just before he moved even deeper into the wilderness. The New Testament thus introduces baptism as no domesticated experience: John's baptism involves a journey away from built-up human civilization, a great river, the edge of wilderness, and a wild baptizer.

Over time, Christian baptisms largely moved indoors. But even as they did, at least some Christians continued to treasure the wild nature of baptismal water. One early Christian document known as the *Didache* gave brief but specific instructions about the baptismal water and baptismal practice:

> Concerning baptism, baptize in this way: after speaking all these words, baptize into the name of the Father, the Son, and the Holy Spirit in living water. If you do not have living water, baptize in other water; if you are not able in cold water, in warm. If you do not have either, pour water on the head three times into the name of the Father, Son, and Holy Spirit.[2]

The *Didache* first lists water that is flowing from a "living" source— "living" in this context means naturally flowing, like a river or stream. And it seems that the *Didache* assumes that the baptismal candidates are *plunged* into this water three times. However, if there were no sufficient pool of living water, another pool of cold water would suffice. Cold water likely would have been most recently "living water," flowing from the earth (and, more practically, would have contained fewer impurities and bacteria). Into this water, again, it seems that the *Didache* preferred that the candidates be *plunged* three times. And yet, if no cold water were available, warmer water (we might think room temperature) would suffice. And yet if no water-pool of suffi-cient size were available, then, the *Didache* counseled, pouring water over the candidate's head three times was appropriate.

In all this specificity there may be wisdom for us today. Baptism may take a number of different forms, and may be enacted with different sets of practices. But, at the same time, the form and shape of the water we use for baptism, and the way in which we baptize, matters. For the *Didache*, it seems that it was important that water clearly flow from the earth, and that a powerful bodily encounter with that water was enabled.

It may be surprising to consider the baptismal practices of the *Didache* and of John the Baptist and to contrast them to one's own congregational baptismal practices. For many of us, there is quite a gap between, on the one hand, the wilderness-pilgrimage baptisms of John and the attention to the "living" character of the water in the *Didache*, and, on the other, what are often the small and hidden—perhaps even dry and covered—baptism-places in many of our wor-ship spaces. Happily, this is changing. Many congregations, especially in the past fifty years as part of the liturgical renewal movement, have been enlarging and strengthening the water-places for baptism in their worship spaces. Congregations seeking to wade deeper into the ecological and theological waters that flow through Psalm 104, the baptismal practices of John the Baptist, and the community of the *Didache*, might consider how their own baptismal water-place might more fully welcome the living nature of Earth's water.

We might think of the eco-theological dimensions of a baptismal water-place in terms of four characteristics: a place of life, an oasis; water that is living, that flows; a place that holds depths of water; and a place that welcomes what we might call the untamed or even wild character of water.

Waters of life: oases
Every living thing on earth depends fundamentally on water. In dry regions, the emergence of fresh water as a spring or a stream on the

landscape typically creates an area that flourishes with life and bio-
logical diversity, perhaps being transformed more dramatically than
surrounding areas as the seasons turn from winter to spring, and
from summer to fall. Such places make clear: from water bursts forth
abundant life. Some congregations celebrate and call attention to the
life-giving ecological character of water by dressing their baptismal
places as oases within their worship spaces. Potted plants and flowers
may be arranged beautifully around the font, perhaps even including
smaller trees, suggesting that the font is an oasis of life, given the way
that baptism gives new life to Christians and how water gives life to
all living things. The baptismal water-place might also show seasonal
changes that reflect the turning of earth's seasons together with the
liturgical year: during Lent, the baptismal area might be dressed with
river stones and perhaps some dry branches, with the growing plants
removed from the baptismal area. At Easter, the baptismal area might
overflow with life, including Easter lilies and flowers of many kinds,
recalling the power of water to give life to parched lands, along with
God's power to bring life out of death on the landscape, in Christ's
death and resurrection, and in our baptisms.

Living water: flowing and pouring

Psalm 104 celebrates the way in which water pours down from above
(the sky, mountains, springs) to below (meadows, valleys, the earth,
the sea). This flowing water serves, in the psalm, as a sign of God's
overflowing blessings on creation, pouring down from God to the
earth and giving life to creatures. Many congregations, when building new worship spaces or remodeling existing ones, are finding ways
for their fonts to carry flowing water—"living water" as the *Didache*
and the Bible describe it. Some fonts have two levels: an upper basin,
perhaps for the baptism of infants, out of which water pours into a
larger pool below, which might be used for the baptism of older children and adults. Some pooled fonts gently circulate water within the
pool, much like a spring, serving as a subtle reminder that water flows

to the font from beyond this place. Some congregations, even while waiting to reform the structure of their fonts, are practicing a more robust pouring of water over the heads of the baptized, perhaps while the minister and the baptized stand in a pool of water set out and adorned specially for a baptismal festival.

In the flowing water at our fonts, we may be reminded of water's flow over the landscape that brings life to the earth and, by its flowing nature, is always being refreshed, always new. We may also be reminded that water flows with a power of its own, and that it comes to us, as one liturgical theologian has written, from "beyond our circle," from places outside of our control.[3] When new Christians are made in flowing baptismal waters, all of these associations—the overflowing blessings of God, the nourishing flow of water over the landscape, the always-new quality of flowing water, and the life-giving power that flows to us from beyond our control—wash over the newly baptized and deepen our appreciation for the significance of baptism.

Scriptural imagery for baptism draws on and resonates with, and seems to welcome, water that flows, that lives. Psalm 65 celebrates that "you visit the earth and water it abundantly; . . . the river of God is full of water. . . . You drench the furrows and smooth out the ridges; with heavy rain you soften the ground and bless its increase" (Ps. 65:9-10). Isaiah exults in the waters flowing to the earth: "waters shall break forth in the wilderness, and streams in the desert . . . as the rain and snow come down from heaven, and do not return there until they have watered the earth, making it bring forth and sprout . . . so shall my word be" (Isa. 35:6; 55:10-11). The prophet Amos calls out to "let justice roll down like waters, and righteousness like an ever-flowing stream" (Amos 5:24). Jesus says to the Samaritan woman at the well, "the water that I will give will become in them a spring of water gushing up to eternal life" (John 4:14). Scripture draws on the life-giving power of flowing water to communicate the goodness and power of God. Our fonts, too, might connect with these texts and the great flowing waters as we let them flow in the midst of our worship spaces.

Pooled waters: mysterious depths

In addition to water flowing and pouring over the landscape, the other prominent way in which we encounter water is in *pooled* water. In addition to rain, streams, rivers, and waterfalls, we also experience water in lakes, pools, ponds, and seas. This pooled state of water on the landscape holds and conserves ecological riches: a source for the clouds that rain down on the land, diverse ecologies on and under the surface for myriads of creatures, space for water-creatures such as whales and giant squid for whom many other bodies of water are too small, a place of refuge for water creatures hiding from others whose home is on land or in the air, and a reservoir of nourishing water that endures and will not simply flow away.

Humans are drawn into such water-depths for, among other things, bathing, exploration, and play. When humans bodily enter deeply pooled water, we often experience it as a surrendering to something larger and more powerful than ourselves. The depths of water have forces of their own— we feel water pressure against our lungs and on our ears, waves and currents move our bodies, and the buoyant force of water keeps us from simply sinking. Deeply pooled water, we know, holds mysteries and dangers: we cannot on our own see into or even approach the hidden depths of lakes or seas. The threats in deep water include both drowning and the hungry creatures who make the deep water their home and hunting ground. At the same time, descending bodily into pooled water is often a euphoric experience of well-being. Whether it is jumping into a cool lake from a rock ledge on a summer day, or rising and falling while floating gently in the waves at a beach, or simply lowering one's body into a still bath after a long day, humans often experience the power of water as a glorification of life and of our bodies. In it we find a deep experience of the goodness of the earth and we may feel immersed in such goodness. In pooled water, we enter all of these things: something larger than ourselves; powers beyond our own; hidden mysteries and dangers; and refreshment that can evoke some of our deepest joys.

Fonts that hold pooled depths enough for our bodies to enter fully evoke on a deep, bodily level the many pooled water-places of the earth. They resonate with theological significance arising from scriptural images of deeply pooled water: the pooled abyss of water, covered in darkness, over which the Spirit broods in the first creation narrative in Genesis 1; the waters of the flood again covering the earth, out of which the earth is reborn (Genesis 6–9); the pooled waters of the Red Sea forming a boundary between slavery and freedom for the Israelites (Exodus 14); the pool of Siloam to which Jesus sends a blind man to wash and be healed (John 9:6-11).

Welcoming the nature of water

At a midnight reception after an urban church's recent baptismal festival at its Easter Vigil, members of the baptismal party and of the whole congregation enjoyed recounting the way in which the "hairdos" of the baptized (both adults and children) were "messed up" by the water poured generously over their heads as they stood in the large font. They joked with each other, smiled and laughed, but they also repeatedly interpreted the funny "messed up hairdos" as a sign of something much deeper: "baptism into Christ is a radical thing; it profoundly rearranges your life." The water, poured out, disrupted the careful grooming and neatness of the baptismal party, as if something of the wilderness baptism of John the Baptist had flowed into that urban Vigil of Easter.

How shall we welcome the living waters of the earth into our worship spaces? What sort of space gives the waters a home in which the waters can show forth their connection to all the living water of the earth? Can we, even within our buildings, glimpse the untamed nature of earth's great waters without which we could not live?

A number of considerations may help us think about our relationship to the earth's water at our baptismal spaces. First, we might simply ask if the assembly can see the water. Many fonts today are designed so that water is the star. Such fonts might be designed with pumps that allow for pouring or flowing water, or they might include a large, wide bowl—perhaps glass, stone, or brass—for holding the water. Some congregations who have inherited and may still treasure an old wooden font-stand in which a small metal bowl was originally inset are now replacing the inset metal bowl with a large glass bowl that is meant to rest only partially in the inset space and thus extends significantly higher than the wooden base; the water in the glass bowl therefore stands beautifully above the base and can be seen by all. Lighting, also, plays a role in how well the water can be seen: is the baptismal area well lit?

Another consideration in welcoming the untamed dimension of the earth's water is the space around the baptismal water. Does it welcome the splashes of water that are inevitably part of a baptism in which water is generously used? Many churches are installing stone or tile flooring around the baptismal font in order to construct a space that invites plentiful use of water and that can help relieve any worries about water on wooden floors or carpeting. A baptism space might also deepen the experience of "untamed" water by providing an area for the assembly to gather around the font for baptisms and for other occasional rites. They may pass by the font to touch the water and perhaps make the sign of the cross as a remembrance of baptism. Bodily proximity to and engagement with the water helps keep the water from being sealed off from the assembly, literally out of touch, and completely tamed. Does the baptismal space create a liturgical center that clearly indicates that baptism—and the water of baptism—*matters* to and is welcomed by this community? In other words, is water given a strong and meaningful place in the worship space?

The materials used in constructing the font also contribute to the sense of the font bearing a basic part of earth and life into the worship space. Materials that recognizably come from the earth and that have been fashioned carefully and minimally by human beings (stone, wood, glass, and ores refined into metals) may attest to the "wild" origins of these materials and of the water itself. For sprinkling baptismal water over the assembly during worship in an act that echoes rain as a remembrance of baptism, an evergreen bough or a brushlike aspergillum made of natural fibers embodies a direct connection to earthly materials. Some congregations, working with an artist, install beautiful pin lights or artistically crafted reflective materials above the font to connect the font's waters with the air, the rain, the heavens. Some congregations might work with a designer to suspend a field of prisms above the font, so that lighting at baptisms might spread the sign of the rainbow through the worship space, the sign of the covenant of care that God made with the whole earth and all its creatures. All of these materials—including the water itself—probably best stand by themselves, without many additional symbols or words physically adorning them. The living word itself—in preaching, prayer, and action—will come to these elements in the act of worship.

Of course, many congregations celebrate baptismal festivals at local bodies of water including lakes, streams, and oceans. These settings may provide a robust encounter with water in its wider ecological setting. Perhaps congregations might schedule a yearly baptismal festival at a local body of water on or around the festival of St. John the Baptist (June 24), a time at which some congregations already hold an annual blessing of the local watercourses.

Praying at the water

At baptisms and other baptismal occasions, the presider prays a prayer of thanksgiving at the water. The prayer of thanksgiving written by Martin Luther is known as the "Flood Prayer." This prayer has been tremendously influential ecumenically and among Lutherans for whom many current baptismal prayers still bear echoes of Luther's 1523 prayer. While the prayer includes other water imagery, Luther adopts the image of Noah's flood as the prayer's central image. Luther, writing elsewhere about baptism as a flood, highlights the global nature of the flood: the entire world is covered; and, while the flood of Noah was what Luther called "a flood of wrath," the flood of baptism is, in Luther's language, "a flood of grace," submerging the entire world in God's mercy.

Luther's prayer did not ask God to change the small pool of water in the font into "holy water," but rather thanked God that, through the baptism of Christ in the Jordan, "the Jordan and *all* water" have been "sanctified and set apart . . . for a saving flood."[4] In other words, for Luther, all the waters in the world are even now part of a saving flood of mercy flowing from God.

Prayers of thanksgiving at the font are prominent in *Evangelical Lutheran Worship*. In addition to the expanded rites of the baptismal process, every Sunday also now includes the option of a thanksgiving for baptism as part of the gathering rite. Thus, many Sundays may include a prayer of thanksgiving at the water, allowing the assembly an opportunity to praise God for the waters of the earth, for the gift of baptism, and to pray for renewal by the power of the Spirit.

Three simple practices seem to draw assemblies deeper into this prayer and into a sense of connection to baptism and to the water itself. Just before the prayer begins, the presider or other ministers are encouraged to pour water into the font, perhaps from a glass pitcher. Assemblies that can hear and see water poured out generously and completely before this prayer begins often speak of an expanded sense of God's generous and complete self-giving in the gift of Jesus, in the sending of the Holy Spirit, in the creation, and in baptism. Thus this pouring probably should be more than a mere trickle of water, but a full, confident, pouring out that resonates and that even can call to mind the "sound of many waters" (Rev. 14:2).

Within the texts of prayers of thanksgiving at the font, a simple interpolation can honor Luther's insistence that *all* water has been made a saving flood, and can connect the biblical and baptismal waters to our local watersheds: we may add a specific local body of water or two to the list of waters for which we give thanks. This practice is clearly laid out in prayer for the Thanksgiving for Baptism in the Pastoral Care volume of *Evangelical Lutheran Worship*, but it may be done with any of the prayers of thanksgiving at the water. One community in Washington State adapted Thanksgiving at the Font V (*Evangelical Lutheran Worship*, 71) for their local watershed:

> Glory to you for oceans and lakes, rivers and creeks. Honor to you for cloud and rain, dew and snow. *Praise to you for Isella Glacier and Railroad Creek, for Lake Chelan and Columbia River.* Your waters are below us, around us, above us: our life is born in you. You are the fountain of resurrection.

As we pray such prayers we will inevitably be reminded of the need for God's protection and healing for these local waters. We may wonder if we should also intercede for these waters and pray for their health in this prayer. This, however, may not be the best occasion for such intercession. This prayer thanks God for blessing us through water and then prays—intercedes—that God will again bless us through the baptismal covenant and its waters. The intercession in this case is for those approaching the baptismal waters and those who have already passed through. The obvious and strong place for interceding for the health and flourishing of water is in the prayers of intercession. In such prayers we typically pray for leaders in government and in the church, and for those who are sick, mourning, or in any need, by name. *Evangelical Lutheran Worship* also specifically encourages us to pray for creation, perhaps adding names of other creatures in need, including specific bodies of water, along with species, forests, mountains, and perhaps other distinct creatures. We should note that we also pray for victims of natural disasters such as floods, storms, drought, and landslides. While today it is the *goodness* and *giftedness* of the earth that Christians and others probably tend to forget more often than the dangerous, pain-inflicting nature of our planet, both characteristics of the earth call us to prayer. In short, at the baptismal waters we give thanks for God's saving and mighty acts known through water, and we pray that the waters of baptism might unite us and hold us in Christ, the living vine and river of life. At the baptismal waters we humans are the needy ones. In the prayers of intercession we intercede for all those in need, including the needy among the wide family of God's creatures, including the waters of the earth.

If this prayer is prayed as part of the gathering rite, *Evangelical Lutheran Worship* suggests the option during the gathering hymn of sprinkling the assembly with water. This action, in addition to the direct physical connection to the baptismal waters, may also suggest connections between rain and the waters of baptism, perhaps encouraging assemblies to come to know rain more fully as a reminder of baptism and as a sign of God's nurturing care for the whole earth. This sprinkling of water in worship, too, seems to evoke in many participants a sense of joy in both the goodness of God and of God's creation, perhaps partly as a deep emotional and embodied response to the nourishing ecological nature of rain.

Come to the waters

Martin Luther famously wrote that in baptism every Christian has enough to learn and to practice for an entire lifetime.[5] This short chapter in this short book obviously leaves most of the dimensions of baptism unexplored. But perhaps some previously unexplored ecological dimensions of baptism have here been opened. In a few glimpses, a wide panorama spreads out: Psalm 104 leads us into a prayer that sees the ecologically flourishing, water-nourished landscape as a glorious sign of God's overflowing blessings on the earth. In baptism we are invited into such vision that sees in the life-giving waters of the earth the promise of God in Jesus Christ by the power of the Holy Spirit. Some ways that we might deepen our appreciation for these ecological dimensions of baptism include attending to our places for baptizing: caring for our baptismal water-places and cultivating life there, letting it take the shape of a seasonally changing oases; shaping baptismal spaces that allow for living, or flowing, water; finding ways for our baptismal spaces to hold true depths of water; and generously, gratefully welcoming water into our worship spaces, and even perhaps celebrating baptismal festivals at local streams, lakes, or oceans. Our prayer of thanksgiving at the water may draw us regularly into thanksgiving for baptism, for all water, and also specifically for our local waters. And, finally, in an age in which many of us are cut off from meaningful engagement with water in ecologically intact and flourishing environments, congregations might, with some regularity, enable encounters with local watersheds, learning their wisdom, caring for their health, and recovering the biblical images of flowing water on the landscape as meaningful language for today's prayer.

In all of humanity's explorations, we have only found flourishing life where the waters are healthy. The images of water that saturate our baptismal theology and prayers are today, in this age of ecological emergency, as needed and relevant as ever before in our history. Our prayer and study at the baptismal waters may thus draw us deeper into the waters that washed with healing over Naaman, that flowed over the psalmist's flourishing landscape, and that flow bright as crystal through the promised city of God beside the healing tree of life (2 Kings 5; Ps. 104; Rev. 22:1-2).

For reflection and discussion

1. Think of a powerful water-place you have visited. How did you experience it in your body? How is your experience there like or unlike an encounter with God?

2. The Evangelical Lutheran Church in America's sacramental practices statement, *The Use of the Means of Grace*, suggests that water be "used generously in Holy Baptism" (Principle 26, p. 31). How could your congregation more fully embody this principle?

3. Have you been to a baptism by immersion? To a baptism in a stream, lake, or ocean? How did you experience these baptisms?

4. Think about your local congregation's baptismal font. In what ways does it suggest connection to the wider waters of God's earth? What is one easy way to strengthen that connection? What is one longer-term way to do so?

5. What is the name of your local watershed? What are its boundaries? To what point does it flow? How healthy is it?

3
Seasons and Days[1]

Easter on Fourth of July?

In Barbara Kingsolver's novel *The Poisonwood Bible*, the Reverend Nathan Price arrives as a Baptist missionary with his family in a remote village in the Belgian Congo in the late 1950s. His time there is fraught with painful, ugly-American blunders: he tries to baptize children in what turns out to be a crocodile-infested river and, perhaps appropriately, even mispronounces the local word for *baptize* in such a way that it comes out meaning not *baptize* but rather *terrorize* ("I want to terrorize your children in the crocodile-infested river in the name of God"). As he encounters for the first time the local calendar based almost solely on a five-day week without any months, he finds himself unable to link the date of Easter to any yearly point meaningful to the local people. So, as his daughter narrates in the novel, because he has arrived in summer and he needs "a focal point to get the church geared up"—he fixes the annual date of Easter in this Central African village as the Fourth of July.[2]

And why not? Perhaps you have had trouble planning for next year's Easter services because Easter falls on a different date each year.

The Fourth of July would make it so much easier. Would anything be lost if we switched Easter to the Fourth of July?

In the first part of this chapter, we will explore how the liturgical year is more than an arbitrary choice of dates, and how it is also something other than our pretending to relive ancient history. We will see how the *great texts of the scriptures* and the *great seasons of the earth* come together in the liturgical year. Contrary to what Rev. Nathan Price said, Easter is not marked on the Fourth of July, but is observed in a much more interesting—and even ecological—way.

Advent

The new liturgical year begins with Advent, the beginning of the Christmas cycle. Call to mind what is happening around us—outside—as we enter Advent. During Advent, roughly the month of December, the nights are growing dramatically longer and the days are growing shorter as the earth's northern hemisphere angles away from the sun and we rotate each day more and more deeply into darkness. The darkness grows deepest at the winter solstice, the longest night of the year. This night is, according to our current calendar, usually the night of December 21, but in the years during which the church's liturgical calendar became set, the winter solstice was marked on another familiar date: December 25. In other words, the date that the church chose for the festival of the incarnation of Christ was also a cosmological hinge-point on the earth and in the sky, the time when the world as the church knew it was draped in deepest darkness. This season often evoked among people of many cultures an ancient fear that the darkness and cold would steadily increase until the world itself came to an end, cloaked in frigid darkness and death.

Next to this darkness and fear about the end of the world, the church set scripture passages for proclamation to itself and to the world. Notice that the passages are not simply about anticipating the birth of Jesus, as if we would be surprised by the announcement of Christ's birth at Christmas. Rather, many of the readings speak to our ecological location in darkness and to the ancient fear of the end of the world—a fear newly rekindled by increasing human ability to destroy. In a dark time and place, the Advent texts proclaim guidance, caution, and promise:

> You know what time it is, how it is now the moment for you to *wake from sleep*. For salvation is nearer to us now than when we became believers; the *night is far gone, the day is near*. Let us then lay aside the works of darkness and put on the armor of light; let us *live honorably* as in the day. (Rom. 13:11-13; emphasis added)

> *There will be signs in the sun, the moon, and the stars, and on the earth distress among nations* confused by the roaring of the sea and the waves. People will faint from *fear and foreboding of what is coming upon the world*. Then they will see 'the Son of Man coming in a cloud' with power and great glory. Now *when these things begin to take place, stand up and raise your heads, because your redemption is drawing near*. (Luke 21:25-28; emphasis added)

> By the tender mercy of our God, the *dawn from on high* will break upon us, to give *light to those who sit in darkness* and in the *shadow of death*, to guide our feet into the way of peace. (Luke 1:78-79; emphasis added)

It is not only ancient peoples for whom the earth's darkness is a matter of spiritual concern. Researchers continue to uncover the powerful physiological effects of long, dark nights on humans, including what is sometimes given the clinical label of "seasonal affective disorder" (SAD). The earth's darkness still exerts its force on us, and, like the ancients who feared the end of the world looming, we too may share such fears, because of the inchoate dread that longer nights can bring on, and also because of what we read in the news.

With the texts and images of Advent, we learn, as our ancestors in faith have learned in ages past, to pray in and with Earth's darkness—both ecological darkness and metaphorical darkness. We raise up the

Advent wreath (perhaps a tradition originating in the hanging-up of wagon wheels in the snowy winter to keep them from warping, on which people lit more and more candles as the darkness grew deeper), and we circle it around with light and hope. The color for Advent is deep midnight blue—the color of a world tilted away from the sun. With our churches draped in midnight blue, with the candles lit against the growing darkness, Advent invites images of hope and expectation in the darkness: the darkness of the winter, of night, of the womb, of the frightened darknesses of our hearts and our world. In Advent we practice waiting and watching for God who comes, as the Advent readings remind us, like a thief in the night. We remember the nighttime dream of Joseph, who is given joy and hope when he despairs. We are told to keep awake, to watch for signs in the darkened sky, that night is far gone and day is near. John the Baptist says that he is not the light but testifies to the light that is coming, the dawn from on high that shall break upon us, who will give light to all who dwell in darkness and the shadow of death. During this season, when we heighten the images of darkness and watchfulness under the starry sky, and drape our space in the deep midnight blue color appointed for the season, the lectionary texts call our attention to the ecological changes all around us on earth. In a sort of duet, the changing season of the earth and the Advent scriptural texts may inspire us to keep awake in times of darkness to watch for Christ's light to dawn and to walk in real and metaphoric darkness with trust in God.

In Advent, the earth's deep darkness serves as a primary sign to which the Word of God speaks. It can be a powerful sign. At my home in Chicago, there are 52 more hours of darkness in each week of Advent than there are during the height of summertime. It is as if the darkness of the natural world poses the question each Advent: how are we to walk in (metaphorical) darkness? And the texts, hymns, colors, and candles of the season proclaim Christ's life-giving way in all our darknesses.

Notice, then, that Advent is not simply an idea that will come and go according to trends or fads. The darkness is the earth's, and we will continue to enter it, year after year. Thus we can see that for Advent, and, indeed, for many of the church's seasons, the organizing pattern of our calendar is not drawn up by a committee or a council, but is rather given to us by the earth, sun, and moon.

As we explore some prominent texts and images from the church's other seasons, notice how the cycles of the earth are a foundational reality in the way that the seasons are marked. Perhaps a renewed attentiveness to the seasons of the church's worship life may lead us deeper into an awareness of the earth's life-giving cycles and our place within them, and, through our worship, help us rediscover how to pray with the earth and its seasons. In Advent, as we will see is true for the other seasons of the church year, the pattern is surprisingly clear: the scriptural texts enter into a dialog with the natural cycles of the seasons. The ecological changes around us resound with scriptural images even as our prayer is drawn outward, approaching our ecological surroundings as living, many-splendored, sacred signs.

Christmas and Epiphany

At the darkest time of the year, Christians celebrate the birth of the Light of the world, Jesus Christ, born in Bethlehem under a star. Still now in our darkness, we celebrate his birth as light dawning on our world again. In our darkness, we speak again those ancient words: *the people who walked in darkness have seen a great light; those who lived in a land of deep darkness, on them light has shined. The true light, which enlightens everyone, has come into the world. In Christ is life, and the life is the light of all people. The light shines in the darkness, and the darkness did not overcome it.*

As the days grow longer again and the nights begin to grow shorter, the twelve days of Christmas and the season after Epiphany exult in the imagery of growing light. Christ's light brings its gifts not only to Christian lives, but, especially in Epiphany, we celebrate the way Christ's light extends to all the corners of the earth: Nations shall come to your light, and kings to the brightness of your dawn (Isa. 60:3).

Christmas is especially suited for hearty celebrations of the light, love, and joy of Christ born into our dark world. Our doctors may encourage us, in the winter darkness, to sit under full spectrum light bulbs to raise our spirits, but another important part of what our spirits need is to celebrate together with others in joyful worship and song the light that no darkness can overcome—the light of Christ.

In medieval Europe, the season after Epiphany sometimes began with everyone carrying their Christmas trees and greenery to the town square or church for a great bonfire, to celebrate that the light of Christ now spreads among the nations. So the season after Epiphany is a little green season, a little growth spurt of the church in winter, a time when we might highlight global connections in our worship through hymnody, art, and offerings, as our texts celebrate the light of Christ spreading among the nations of the world. The Epiphany texts call out to our land, emerging from winter darkness: Arise, shine; for your light has come, and the glory of the LORD has risen upon you (Isa. 60:1).

Keeping communion with the southern hemisphere

While this book is written for a North American context, it is important to note that the cycles of the seasons are more or less reversed in the southern hemisphere: the dark winter solstice in the northern hemisphere is the peak of summer sunlight in the southern hemisphere. This raises a number of questions for liturgical practice. In this global age, three gifts seem to come of this dilemma. First, it is largely Christians in the southern hemisphere who have called attention to the deep connections between the church year and the cycles of the earth—partly because they have experienced how some prayers and hymns seem oddly out of place in their lands. Therefore, elegantly, it has been in fact Christians in the southern hemisphere who have been reminding northern hemisphere Christians about the deep connections between the ecological and liturgical year, naming these connections as gifts for those in the northern hemisphere, encouraging those of us in the North to draw more deeply on them. Second, Christians in the southern hemisphere have found ways to highlight seasonal imagery in the church's calendar of readings that is appropriate for the southern hemisphere. The light and darkness images of the Christmas cycle do in fact resonate with the long days of light in the southern hemisphere, and the summertime fields seem to rejoice in the festival of the incarnation; Easter in Australia comes at the end of the dry summer, and thus the renewing rains of Easter call to mind the promise of God's renewal even to the land.[3] Third, Christians in the northern hemisphere do well intentionally to keep communion with the southern hemisphere. Our prayers of intercession might pray for other communities in their own times of harvest, monsoon, or summer heat. Sermons might draw on the different dimensions of a scripture text if it were heard within the seasonal surroundings of the southern hemisphere. Members of our congregations from the southern hemisphere might discuss their seasonal liturgical traditions in an adult forum. (Those Christians who live near the equator experience relatively small changes in the length of day and night over the course of a year. Thus, the primary ecological cycle with which liturgy engages for those near the equator may be the daily cycle of sunrise and sunset, night and day.) By knowing our own local ecological cycles as sacred signs for liturgy—even as we keep communion with others in very different ecological cycles— we discover ways for Christians to live into the dual citizenship that seems to be a healthy part of modern ecological awareness: engagement with both the local and the global.

Lent

The season of Lent, in some ways, was the early church's solution to the need for a period of baptismal preparation, which culminated with the baptisms of individuals and families at the Easter Vigil. Sometimes we think of Lent only as a time to feel bad about our sins or to mourn Jesus' death for five weeks. While Lent is indeed serious about sin and does in fact prepare us to enter the mystery of the death and resurrection of Christ at Easter, Lent is also true to its DNA when we use it to prepare for and to be refreshed by the waters of baptism.

We begin Lent on Ash Wednesday, being reminded that we in our bodies are made of earth, and to earth we shall return. St. Augustine said that our bodies are "the earth we carry." For a while, this earth rises up, speaks, walks, and sings. To this earth, Lent adds *water*, the waters of late winter and spring rains, the water of baptism. When earth is nourished with living water, when our bodies are bathed in the living water of Christ, the living earth (of the ground, of ourselves) grows and bears fruit. During the weeks of Lent, the landscape comes alive with the year's most vigorous period of growth. Even the desert in the American Southwest begins to bloom. In the fourth century, Ambrose of Milan preached to those baptized at Easter, "you were dry, and you began to flower again in the abundant waters of the font," and, like a tree, "you were 'planted by streams of water' and 'began to bring forth fruit.'"[4]

Cyril of Alexandria, in the fifth century, looked around at the blossoming earth at Easter and wrote that "it would be truly unthinkable that all growing plants and all kinds of trees regain their original appearance, while the people . . . should lie destitute of the care of heavenly providence."[5] Many in the early church saw baptism at springtime as the human way of being renewed—like a garden watered at springtime and bearing forth abundant fruit.

The lectionary readings overflow with water images during Lent: the rainbow covenant with Noah, the baptism of Jesus, the Samaritan woman at the well, Nicodemus learning about being born of water and the spirit, the promised land that will stretch "from the River of Egypt to the great river, the river Euphrates," water from the rock in the wilderness, rivers in the desert, a way through the sea, Israel's exodus likened to a baptism in the sea, and Isaiah's call for everyone who thirsts to "come to the waters."

The purple color of Lent, the color of deep, dark, watery depths, adorns the worship space, perhaps even with suggestions of water ripples or waterfalls or ocean depths in some of our paraments and art. The font might be highlighted by gathering each Sunday at the water, pouring water generously into it, and perhaps surrounding the font with river stones or beautiful images and elements from the desert, making the font a little oasis in the forty days of the wilderness of Lent.

Easter

Just as the Christmas cycle pivots around the winter solstice, so too does Easter find an anchor in the signs of earth and heaven. Easter's signs, however, are considerably more complex. Easter is kept on the Sunday after the first full moon following the spring equinox. That is indeed a complex formula for us to sort out today. Far from being as simple as Rev. Nathan Price's Fourth of July, as we watch for the coming of Easter, we attend to a number of ecological and cosmic signs: first we watch for the coming of spring, the season of the most robust change and growth on the landscape. Then we wait for the spring equinox, the time at which the plane of the earth's equator directly intersects the sun, so that day and night are held in balance around the entire world. Following the spring equinox, we watch for the full moon. (This full moon marks the Jewish festival of Passover, the time of Jesus' passion, according to the scriptures. The cosmic signs associated with Passover, however, are now, for complicated reasons, sometimes calculated differently in Christian and Jewish practice.) Under the light of a bright moon, Christians wait for Sunday to begin—it is both the day of Christ's resurrection in the gospels and the first day of creation in the Genesis 1 narrative. Some Jews and early Christians, inspired by the springtime renewal of the land and the people, even kept oral traditions that suggested that the cosmos was itself created on Easter/Passover. And while day is often reckoned as beginning with sunrise or midnight in North America, in the Jewish tradition and in the classic Christian tradition, day begins with nightfall. So Easter itself is liturgically marked beginning with sundown on Saturday: the Easter Vigil.

All of these signs—springtime, equinox, full moon, Sunday, and night—may seem archaic or irrelevant to many of us. Most of us, today, when planning for Easter, do not look to the earth and the heavens but to a numbered grid of boxes—our modern calendar— and look for the box labeled Easter. And in this age of digital calendars and clocks, we can, in fact, communicate the timing of Easter in purely digital code: 3-31-2013. With such technology, Easter could be calculated in a bunker deep under the ground—completely cut off from the cycles of the earth's own renewal.

However, what may seem quaint to some today was vitally important to some of our ancestors in faith. St. Augustine himself contrasted the relatively simple fixed date of Christmas to what he called the sacramental nature of Easter's cosmic and ecological time-keeping signs. One early preacher specifically named springtime, equinox, full moon, nighttime, and Sunday, and proclaimed that "the Pascha [Easter] cannot be celebrated when one of these elements is missing . . . by putting all of these occurrences together, we reveal the inner meaning of the saving passion."[6] Even as we may disagree with the claim that Easter *cannot* be celebrated apart from these signs, this early preacher's insistence on the theological significance of these ecological and cosmic signs may cause us to wonder about what dimension of Easter's significance we may be missing if we only attend to the numbers and grids of our calendars and clocks at Eastertime.

The Easter Vigil liturgy is resonant with images of the earth and the cosmos being renewed in God and in the resurrection of Christ. The service normally begins outdoors under the night sky, with the assembly gathered around a fire newly struck in the darkness. This basic act connects the mystery of fire to the rekindled, risen life of Christ out of death. Thus, this new fire at the Easter Vigil may serve as our most meaningful encounter with fire throughout the year and so may reorient our relationship to fire, such that we come to approach it sacramentally, approaching even the act of *burning* as rightly done only in mercy, only for the renewal of God's world. In some cultures, after the Easter vigil, flames from this new fire are carried home to light the home hearth—even to relight stoves, furnaces, and pilot lights—so that the fire that gives heat and light to the home throughout the year is the new fire of Easter, the light of Christ.

From the new fire a great candle is lighted and brought into the worship space. The thanksgiving prayer for the light of the candle is an adapted version of an ancient prayer that gives thanks for the resurrection's renewal of the whole cosmos, from the stars of heaven to the bees who have given wax for the candle, to the earth, to the assembly gathered in the candlelight. "This is the night," the prayer sings out, "in which heaven and earth are joined."

The vigil readings resound with images of creation being restored by the power of God: the story of creation in Genesis 1; the renewal of creation and the covenant with the earth in the story of Noah's flood; the word of God likened to rain and snow watering the earth and bringing forth fruit in Isaiah 55; a valley of death and dry bones being restored to flourishing life; with the final reading traditionally being followed by a version of the Benedicite Omnia Opera (for example, ELW 835, "All creatures worship God most high") that repeatedly calls out to the whole creation to join in singing praise to God.

Certainly, something much larger than springtime happens at Easter. In the resurrection of Christ, by the power of God, love conquers hate, gentleness overcomes violence, sin is washed away by mercy, life vanquishes the power of death. And yet, Jesus, who had rested in the earth on the Sabbath, rises to life, according to the Gospel of John, in a garden in the springtime. Jesus had earlier imaged his death as a seed falling into the earth, bearing much fruit. Some early Christians even faithfully imagined Jesus' body resting in the tomb on the Sabbath as his presiding over a cosmic Sabbath of the whole earth, with the entire earth laying in sabbath rest, until, as in a new creation, Christ arose on Sunday, the day of creation, calling the entire creation back to abundant life.

Some newly baptized early Christians celebrated their first Easter eucharist with, in addition to the cup of wine, a cup of milk and honey, a sign that they had arrived in a fertile promised land, a land flowing with milk and honey. A resurrection in a garden, a land flowing with milk and honey, the earth bearing the fruit of life and mercy for which God had created it: can our worship spaces during Easter celebrate this abundant goodness of God? If our fonts were oases during Lent, they can explode with flowers, blooms, and growing green plants at Easter. Our communion tables can be surrounded by signs of a feast in the land of milk and honey: more flowers, vines and branches, beautiful loaves of fresh bread, perhaps food offerings for the hungry in baskets surrounding the table. The color for the season of Easter is white, like the blooms of so many plants in what has become the resurrection garden of the whole earth.

Easter is not just a day, but also a season. It is a week of weeks, seven times seven, to make fifty days of rejoicing, stretching all the way to Pentecost. Our church spaces, our prayers and hymns, give space and time for us to celebrate deeply this gift of the resurrection of Christ, the living one who lives with us now, and still breathes springtime life into our suffering world.

Day of Pentecost

Pentecost sweeps in like an early summer wind that blows wherever it pleases, like tongues of fire—and suddenly a diversity of people catch the gift of the Spirit: "Your sons and your daughters shall prophesy, your young men shall see visions, and your old men shall dream dreams. Even upon my slaves, both men and women, in those days I will pour out my Spirit; and they shall prophesy" (Acts 2:17-18; Joel 2:28-29).

The Day of Pentecost is a time to dress the church in wind and flame: flame-colored streamers in the procession might catch the wind as they move above the assembly. The dove, a symbol of the Spirit, may show up in art and imagery on this day, even as birds make their summer migrations, gathering and hovering over streams and bodies of water. The fiery heat of summer, the power and unpredictability of the wind, the grace and flight of the birds over the water: all these are signs of the Spirit that mark the day of Pentecost.

Summer

After the day of Pentecost the long summer green season begins. It is sometimes called Ordinary Time, or the Sundays after Pentecost. Green is the liturgical color appointed for this growing season. The church, in this long season, has mostly avoided vivid seasonal imagery, and rather has let the scripture readings unfold a little more slowly and naturally, one text after another.

During the summer in year B of the lectionary, we do, however, enter a little season of five weeks for the bread of life passages from the Gospel of John. This can be an opportunity to dress our liturgical spaces with signs of the wheat harvest, of the goodness of bread, of the abundance of manna that God gives to a hungry world.

And, at the end of this long summer time after Pentecost, while it isn't completely a season unto itself, the month of November does have a different character to it: the end of the summer heat, the harvesting of crops, and some preparation for the dying-down of winter. November begins with All Saints Day, holding in memory those who have died, and who now rest in the earth and in God. In the United States there is the national holiday of Thanksgiving with all its harvest motifs, and the lectionary lifts up harvest images as signs of the final ingathering of God's people. The liturgical year ends with Christ the King, or Reign of Christ Sunday, which helps us see Christ again as the ruler of all things, the gentle wounded one among us who is also the lord of all creation. So at the end of the long season after Pentecost, during the season of harvest and dying-down in much of the country, the liturgical year reminds us of the promise of life in the face of endings and death.

Praying with the earth throughout the year

Throughout the sweep of a year, then, Christians learn in worship to read scripture and pray along with the earth in its seasons. The two great festival cycles of Christmas and Easter each have their own character and draw on different aspects of our experience of earth's changing seasons. In the Christmas cycle, scriptural images of darkness and light animate our worship. The growing darkness culminates in our celebration of the birth of Christ our light, and leads to the feast of Epiphany as the light returns, grows, and spreads. The Easter cycle begins with the bare ground of late winter or early spring, reminding us of our identity as earth, as dust, on Ash Wednesday. To this dust, as spring rains fall on the bare earth, are added images of water through the season of Lent, a season of baptismal preparation and recommitment. The season's culmination comes with the confluence of a number of cosmic and ecological signs of God's renewing power: the coming of spring, the earth's days and nights in balance, the bright circle of the full moon, and the night that commemorates both Christ's resurrection and the first day of creation. Standing inside of all of these signs, in the light of newly struck fire, Christians tell their most powerful stories and celebrate the most prominent baptismal festival of the year. The Easter Vigil leads into fifty days of rejoicing as the earth itself is renewed by the power of the resurrection, becoming a springtime garden in which the newly baptized walk. Easter comes to an end at the beginning of summer, with Pentecost's rushing wind and tongues of fire, as the summer heat blows over the land.

So the liturgical year offers what we might call a sacramental approach to the earth's seasons, approaching the earth's great cycles as holy signs of God's saving action in history, drawing us into worship alongside the whole living earth. Our hymns and prayers, the way we dress our worship spaces, our patterns for baptizing, our scripture texts and preaching all are carried out in dialog with the earth and its seasons.

Daily prayer

Seasons, of course, are not the only prominent ecological cycles of the earth that we experience. On a daily basis we know the sun's rising and setting as we rotate into and out of the sun's light, and into and out of our galaxy's star-spangled darkness. Christians, drawing on our Jewish heritage, have prayed along with these daily cycles, too, knowing the daily rhythm of earth and sun and sky as a holy sign and as a partner in prayer to God. (It may be that this daily cycle is a more prominent cyclical pattern for prayer among assemblies closer to the equator, where the rhythms of day and night remain strong, but the seasonal shifts are much less dramatic.) *Evangelical Lutheran Worship* follows a long tradition in commending for prayer especially three occasions.

Morning prayer

How many sunrises have you experienced in your life—the entire sunrise: from dark night, to the earliest hint of dawn, to the rising of the sun over the land? Perhaps you have known such a sunrise while running, or while working farmland, or while camping, or on a long-distance journey, or perhaps at the end of a long night of worry. At the hour of sunrise on Earth, we may find ourselves before a magnificent event in which the creation seems to come again to life with birds and land animals and insects breaking into movement and song with the dawning, the clouds dressed in colored splendor, and plants reaching out toward the sun. This event of morning, today often hidden or missed because of changed cultural patterns of lighting, architecture, busyness, and technology use, is honored in Christian liturgical tradition as an event at which to pray.

For Christians, the beginning of each new day is alive with images that speak of Christ's resurrection and of God's creation of the world—both the first creation and the first-born of the new creation. The songs of morning prayer give thanks to God for these gifts. The opening psalm in *Evangelical Lutheran Worship* (300) echoes with creation imagery:

> In your hand are the caverns of the earth;
> the heights of the hills are also yours.
> The sea is yours, for you made it;
> and your hands have molded the dry land.

Prayed under a morning sky, everything around us seems to join in singing this psalm. Yet even when prayed in a closed building, or silently on a train or bus commuting to work, or even sitting in a cubicle, the psalm invites our spirit to praise God with the wide expanse of the earth. Other morning hymns celebrate the goodness of the earth and give thanks for God's creative and restorative power. For example, a lovely tune from the Philippines is paired with a text that celebrates God's renewing power over the whole earth each morning: "Lord, your hands have formed this world, every part is shaped by you— water tumbling over rocks, air, and sunlight: each day's signs that you make all things new" (ELW 554). The song of Zechariah, the traditional canticle of morning prayer, associates this particular day's dawn with the promised "dawn from on high" that "shall break upon us."

Morning prayer may conclude, especially on festive occasions, with a thanksgiving for baptism. This rite, particularly at morning prayer, gives thanks for the power of Christ's resurrection to make all things new. Standing in the morning at the waters of the font, on land refreshed by its nighttime rest, we pray that we, with the whole earth, may be drawn deeper into the creating and resurrecting power of God that washes over us in baptism, that we, too, might have abundant life like a watered garden, like trees planted by water.

Evening prayer

Many of us make the transition from daylight into evening and sunset with the flip of a light switch. However, from the beginning of civilization until the invention of the incandescent light bulb around 100 years ago, humans necessarily made this transition with considerably more effort and intentionality: as Earth turned away from the sun and the sun's light faded, lamps, torches, fires, or candles were lighted so that light might be carried into the evening's growing darkness.

Early Christians began associating this daily act and the kindled lights themselves with the light of Christ that accompanies us into the darkness. Thus in the daily prayer of some Christians, the lighting of lamps became extended and deliberate, even hallowed, and became a time set aside especially for prayer.

Today's services of evening prayer carry to us in the twenty-first century a long-practiced way of attending prayerfully to Earth's turning into sunset and shadow. The opening of evening prayer may begin with what is known as the service of light, in which, typically, modern electric lights are left dimmed or turned off, and like our ancestors, we light candles for our evening light. As a great candle is carried in procession, a dialogue is sung between the leader and the assembly, weaving together the images of Earth's turn toward night, the enduring light of Christ, and God's loving care for the world. Each season, in fact, has its own dialogue, reflecting the season's particular patterns of light. During Advent, as the candle is carried into the deepening darkness around the winter solstice, we pray: "The whole creation pleads: Amen. Come, Lord Jesus." During the Easter season of springtime, we sing of the risen Christ shining on the world: "We are illumined by the brightness of his rising. Alleluia, alleluia, alleluia!"

As we sing a hymn to Christ the light, many more candles, including, perhaps, tapers held by the assembly, may be lighted in the growing darkness. Following the hymn, the leader may sing a prayer at the burning candle in thanksgiving for light. The shape of this prayer draws on the form of Jewish and Christian prayers of blessing, and thus might be prayed before the candle, with arms outstretched in the *orans* posture, embodying the reverence for the evening light implied in the texts and prayers of the service.

Night prayer

There are some strands of Christian tradition that use images of battle to describe the relationship between light and darkness, life and death. Night prayer as we have received it is largely not part of that tradition. Rather, night prayer generally welcomes darkness as a natural, ecological part of the day. Correlatively, this service can also allude to the natural inevitability of death, for which night prayer asks the peace of God's presence.

The simple, single-line opening prayer of the service sings the basic hope of the entire service: "Almighty God grant us a quiet night and peace at the last." The readings, hymns, and prayers of this service invite us to seek peace with the darkness and night rather than fight against it. Such a piety is counter-cultural in an age that now often floods the night with lights, screens, travel, and digital chatter. Night prayer, from within our busy culture of consumption and hyper-reality, is a treasury of prayer for a people—and an earth—that need rest, sabbath, from such frenetic and often destructive activity.

Evening hymns may be sung at a number of points within the service, and quite a few such hymns are suitable for both evening prayer and night prayer. Many of these hymns approach evening and night with a sacramental sensibility, seeing in the land and sky signs of God's care, peace, and gentle, ongoing creative action. These hymns help us re-enter our world as a wondrous, good home made by God. They sing of shadows resting on "woodland, field, and meadow" ("Now rest beneath night's shadow," ELW 568), while above, "choirs of stars appearing hallow the nightfall" ("Christ, mighty Savior," ELW 560). Some of these hymns image Christ as a nesting bird sheltering creatures from harm (see "When twilight comes," ELW 566). An elegant set of images drawing on the spherical nature of the turning earth animates the hymn "The day you gave us, Lord, has ended" (ELW 569). Even as those who sing this hymn prepare to rest and sleep, this hymn thanks God for the ongoing prayers of those who will soon awake to the rising sun. At all times, as planet Earth turns through space, "each continent and island" takes up the prayer: "The sun, here having set, is waking your children under western skies, and hour by hour, as day is breaking, fresh hymns of thankful praise arise."

Ancient patterns in a new era

The winter's deep darkness and dawning light; the landscape's lively renewal in springtime; the earth's rhythm of sunrise, sunset, and night that orients our body and is literally part of our DNA: these ecological cycles are reflected in the structure of Christian prayer through most of our history. Our ancient prayer practices may help us face a new era today, when our old and partly forgotten patterns of connection to God's earth through prayer may ring out anew, like the chorus of creatures greeting the rising sun at the coming of spring.

For reflection and discussion

1. Which ecological season is your favorite? Why? What scriptural images stand out to you during the simultaneous liturgical season?
2. How does the increased darkness of the winter season affect you?
3. What are your childhood associations with the season of Lent?
4. What sort of shift would it mean for you to enter Lent as a season of baptismal renewal, praying together with the springtime earth for renewal?
5. How might you pray at morning, evening, and night? What sorts of practices, informed by the church's tradition of daily prayer, are possible at home, at work, while commuting? What sorts of practices are possible with family, friends, the congregation?

4
Fields and Vineyards[1]

Food, in worship, leads to God and to the earth

A recent newspaper article portrayed a remote tribal culture as exotic because it still depended directly on the land for its food. The article intended to differentiate this tribe from modern cultures, but instead demonstrated modern culture's everyday obliviousness to where *all* food comes from. Of course, all food, in any culture, comes from the earth and its lands, skies, and waters. Christian scriptures and liturgical texts tend to have a heightened awareness of this reality because our heritage extends back to times (not so long ago) when most people encountered the connection between land and food on a daily basis, often as part of their daily work on the land. But even more profoundly, the Christian tradition honors the connection between food and the land because it is God who has made the land, who makes it fruitful, and who is the one to whom we owe thanks for the gifts of food and drink. And more, among the most profound mysteries that we confess is that Christ comes to us in food, in the bread and wine of holy communion. At communion, in worship, then, *food* is a connection both to God and to the earth.

"As the grains of wheat once scattered on the hill"

I served as pastor to a community that is connected to the wider world (and its sources of food) only by way of a relatively unusual journey. Holden Village, a Lutheran retreat center, is tucked into a steep, mountainous valley in the Pacific Northwest near Canada, surrounded by wilderness. No outside roads reach the village, so the only route for food delivery is by boat up a long wilderness lake, and then by one of the village trucks, up an 11-mile gravel road. When shipments of food arrived in the fall before the long winter months, the entire village gathered to unload the truck, passing the food like a bucket brigade from the truck into our large food lockers. We watched dried cranberries go by, wheels of cheese, great bags of wheat flour, cases of wine, crates of apples grown just down lake, and bananas grown half a world away.

The tenuousness of that link with the outside world—considering that huge snow avalanches sometimes covered and cut off our road to the lake (and the boat)—made clear our connection to and dependence on others distant from us. In the deep of winter, surrounded by many feet of snow and towering, rocky mountains, we were aware that food did not come from grocery stores but from fields and groves of trees and farms quite unlike our surroundings.

One autumn I visited friends across the lake—former villagers—who, in a single weekend, took me to a grape crush and wine tasting at a small, local vineyard, and then to the high-desert farm where wheat for our village bread—including our eucharistic bread—was grown organically. One might call such a journey a *field trip* and emphasize its educational benefits, as I did learn many facts about who grows the food we enjoy in the village, where it is produced, and how it travels to us. That is not insignificant information. Yet something much more profound than information-as-data-intake occurred on that trip. Something more like wonder arced out between the fields, the vineyards, my mind, and the liturgical celebrations of my community. I could now imagine the very particular land on which our bread had been "scattered over the hills and was gathered together and became one," in the words in which the *Didache* encourages us to pray. In the vineyard, I had seen how the branches that abided in the vine bore much fruit, as John remembers Jesus teaching (John 15:1-11). Images of care, labor, and worth associated with vineyards in scripture were now filled out by the bodily experience of the hard and hurried work we did to bring in the precious, fragile grapes. In what was certainly a brief encounter with field and vineyard, my own eucharistic participation and prayer were enriched by encountering *biblical* and *liturgical* images and experiences that were, in fact, unavailable to me within the boundaries of the Sunday liturgy itself.

It was clear, even in this short visit, that the wine and wheat that would feed us in our eucharist across the lake were carried along to us by complex associations of people, land, ecology, politics, and economics. I remember the vintner making calculations involving recent rainfall, air temperature, sugar concentrations in the fruit, sun exposure, soil conditions, time of day, and the taste of the grape in order to determine when exactly to pick the grapes for the crush. To make wine for eucharist *someone* needs to stretch their mind and body outward toward a view of the whole landscape, encompassing an intricate vision of soil, water, sun, sugars, plants, air, rotation of the earth, and the subtleties of human taste. The wheat farm, with its commitment to traditional organic farming methods over and against synthetic industrial production, occupied a social, ecological, and political location that made clear that there is no neutral or abstract way of farming. The family who farms that high desert land makes choices that affect the water quality below them, the health of the animals who live on and near their farm, and those who will eat the wheat they produce. And, even on the remote land where they farm, they are part of the world-wide movement of organic farming in which, every year, more farmers are committing to sustainable farming practices in reaction to the destructive and unsustainable practices of much of industrialized agriculture. Clearly, the food and drink gathered for communion each week are carried along a meaningful path through profound ecological systems and human labor on the way to the table.

Food, land, and relationships

Some congregations are establishing relationships with nearby small, sustainable vineyards who supply them with wine for their eucharist. The same could be true for a supply of wheat. What would it mean for leaders of liturgies to spend time in preparing soil, planting, irrigating, and harvesting on farms that produced the gifts of the earth, the fruit of the vine, and work of human hands for the church's table? Our world is undergoing dizzying changes in economic globalization, climate change, and widespread ecological disruption. In the midst of these changes, members of a congregation—from youth to adult—may come to be settled and at home on land in which the whole cycle from planting to harvesting, from earth to eucharistic table, is visible, comprehensible, and seen in light of the one who opens the hand and gives food to every living thing. Such attentiveness to an event already named in our eucharistic prayers would more than ever bring the world into our liturgical prayer and bring our liturgical prayer into the world.

In one congregation, the worship committee meets occasionally at the local wine shop. The owner goes out to the front window and turns over the sign to read "closed" to those outside, and he spreads a table for them, bringing out a selection of wines produced in their local region, and together, with little tastes of all these wines, the committee asks the question together: what should Easter taste like this year? And then more questions: What about Pentecost? Christmas? Tasting and naming the theological themes of the lectionary, they choose the wines for the upcoming festivals and seasons. Perhaps a port for Advent. A festive champagne for Easter Vigil. Together with the bakers in the congregation they do the same with bread recipes, tasting different recipes and choosing a style of bread for each season. While attention to the taste and feel of the food for communion could certainly be overdone and even *reverse* the meaning of the communion meal toward consumerism or elitism, reverent and faithful care for the selection and preparation of communion food and drink may be part of a wider care and reverence for the earth, and of a deepened reverence for the one who bestows these gifts to us. Such attentiveness—often washed out by mechanization and mass production of food—may help us, along with our ancestors in faith, "taste and see that the LORD is good" (Ps. 34:8).

The ecology of just eating

There is, at the communion table itself, a sort of ecology in the sharing of the meal. One theologian has called it "the economic proposal of the eucharist."[2] Communion is a meal, given by God, in which there is enough for all, with limits on our consumption. All are welcomed to this meal in Christ's name, and the meal is to be shared so that all are fed. This is a peculiar sort of table etiquette that suggests a specific kind of ecology in the way we share in God's nourishing gifts from the land.

When Jesus sat down at table with people in his day, those gathered around the table with him, historians tell us, had an average life expectancy of around 30 years. There were a number of factors: disease and violence were common. But, for 90 percent or so of the population, hunger and malnutrition—food insecurity—were serious threats. So when Jesus called people together at table, many people came hungry. Whether it was Jesus cooking breakfast for disciples whose nets kept coming up empty, or a crowd of thousands gathered on a hillside, or a smaller gathering in an upper room, part of what drew people to table with Jesus was a widespread, underlying, real hunger. Such hunger, we have seen, has a direct connection to the patterns by which human societies relate to the land and its produce.

Today in North America, millions of people are suffering from hunger. More than 10 million people in the United States frequently eat too little or go without a meal, sometimes for an entire day, because they cannot afford adequate food. But in some ways we might think of the situation in North America as being the reverse of the situation in Jesus' day. In Jesus' day, the health of around 90 percent of the population was threatened by a lack of a dependable food supply, while today in North America, the health of around 90 percent of the population is threatened by a supply of food so abundant that our bodies are simply being overwhelmed by it and shutting down. In Jesus' day, the threat that faced many people as they came to the table was serious hunger. And in our day, as we come to the table to eat, the threat that faces many of us in North America is the *absence* of a healthy kind of hunger.

So as we approach this table set with food week after week, we might approach it in the spirit of a well-known table prayer: *Lord, to those who hunger, give bread. And to those who have bread, give hunger for justice.* For many of us in this time and place today, the sharp hunger we feel at the table might first of all be a hunger for justice. And we might also recognize that the real physical hunger that many carry to the table in North America and around the world is also, in fact, a hunger for justice.

Christians confess that the eucharistic feast extends beyond our little assemblies to join other tables across great distances and even across time, and therefore the hungry who gather at eucharistic tables anywhere also join us at our table, in all our gatherings. The ecology of the eucharist that proclaims enough for all, with limits on our consumption, therefore calls us to examine the way in which our food is produced and shared across the great boundaries of the earth.

In Jesus Christ, the bread that we break is never simply "my bread." Just before we eat together, we pray, not "give me today *my* daily bread," but "give us today *our* daily bread." When the words at communion are spoken to us, "the body of Christ, given for you . . . the blood of Christ, given for you," we can miss the second person *plural* of the original Greek text. The Southern tradition can speak the actual grammatical sense of the announcement clearly: "body of Christ, given for y'all . . .

blood of Christ, shed for y'all." We might think back over the centuries and millennia to imagine the many individuals to whom these words have been spoken as the bread has been handed to them, often with the wide intent of the words hidden just below the surface: "given for you all, given for all of you." The medieval mystic Meister Eckhart is purported to have looked at such bread and said, "There is no such thing as 'my' bread. All bread is ours, and given to others through me, and to me through others."[3] The economic proposal of the eucharist is also an ecological proposal: enough for all, with limits on consumption; the produce of the land is shared for Christ's sake, as the land itself is drawn by the power of God into participation in the renewal of human society and the earth itself.

Feeding the multitudes, with baskets left over

Some congregations, as part of their offering, bring forward not only money but also baskets of food items to be shared with the hungry poor. Some congregations even include fresh produce from home, community, and church gardens, allowing the hungry to taste the goodness of the land as they receive gifts given in Christ's name. Such signs are not for self-congratulation, but may challenge us as individuals and as a church to place our treasure where we would like our hearts to be—with God's beloved people, feeding hungers and healing the world—a place where Christ has promised to meet each of us as one of the hungry and needy ones. Perhaps such offerings may give us faith that such goodness and grace will extend also to us in our own difficult times.

At least one congregation sometimes reverses the typical prominence of the money offerings and food offerings, and gives the food offering the most prominent place. The food and money gifts are brought forward to the table where great baskets surrounding it are quickly filled, most visibly with food. And those who also give money drop little dollar bills, coins, checks, or envelopes into the baskets, and watch the money find its home among the cans of vegetable soup and the boxes of potato flakes and the jars of sauerkraut and tomatoes.

The big baskets of food literally put the money offerings into perspective: the offering is given for those who have not been afforded access to adequate fertile land or harvest.

As part of the sending rite of holy communion, bread and wine may be carried to those who are absent from the gathering—those who are homebound, in prison, in nursing homes, or in the hospital. In this ancient and profound act, we extend the goodness that God gives through the land and in the meal to those who are unable to gather with the full assembly. We might see in the path marked across the land from the gathered community to those absent a little sign of God's work in the healing of our relationship with our place, connecting the absent and needy with the prayers of the community, knit together through the bread and wine that is both the fruit of the land itself and the body and blood of Christ. Such a procession may carry other food items, too, to the absent, needy members of the assembly, and to the wider community in need of food.

Approaching the earth's table in gratitude

The earliest Christians, knowing significantly more hunger than most of us in North America today, had a number of names for the gathering they shared around the meal eaten in the name of Christ. One of the classic and enduring names by which these often-hungry people came to know their gathering for worship was simply *eucharist*, which translates *thanksgiving*. This disposition of thanksgiving was understood as being so much a part of the Christian meal that it could become simply the name by which the gathering was known.

Writer Mary Jo Leddy suggests that this disposition of thanksgiving—of prayerful gratitude to God—is of special relevance in an age of ecological emergency in which our ecological problems are deepened by the voracious consumption of resources, mostly by those who have far more than enough shelter, food, and possessions. Gratitude to God as a practice of prayer and life leads to a profound sort of freedom in realizing that God has given us more than enough for life abundant. In a life rooted in prayerful thanksgiving, she writes, "rather than wasting away from a fundamental sense of dissatisfaction with oneself, a person can begin to realize that the life he or she has been given is *enough* to begin with, *enough* to go on . . . As we set some limits on the spirit of craving and dissatisfaction which holds us captive there is an almost simultaneous liberation of a new sense of power."[4] She writes that the power of such gratitude is at the heart of the Christian life, enacted in holy communion:

> The Eucharist has become the great way of thanksgiving. It is the way in which we take our small and sometimes half-hearted acts of gratitude and join them with the total act of thanksgiving that Jesus was and is among us. He lived continually in the recognition that he had been born of God, that he was a child of God, and thus his life became a giving, a giving thanks, a blessing. In him our gratitude becomes whole, holy.[5]

In the great thanksgiving, the prayer of blessing prayed at the eucharistic table, the presider—and among some congregations today, members of the assembly—raises his or her hands in the ancient Christian posture of prayer, the *orans* posture. With hands outstretched, the body language suggests a yielding of the prayer to God, in overwhelmed thanksgiving, and perhaps also speaking of overwhelming need. The great thanksgiving, in fact, does pray for everything. It begins with the creation of the cosmos and the making of earth as our home, continues through the liberation of the people of Israel, recounts the ministry of Jesus and his meals and life-giving passion among us, prays for the coming of the Spirit, and looks forward to the promised day in which God will be all in all, making all things new.

This prayer is one of the most ancient and important ways that Christians have approached, in fact, *everything* in prayer. At Christ's word, the communion table is set for the whole people of the earth, and is set with the gifts of the earth itself. At such a table our needs may become obvious: our injustices and hungers, including our degradations to the fertile land, and our entrenched patterns of eating too much among some and, among others, being left with far too little. And yet, the entire prayer is the great *thanksgiving*, prayed in gratitude for the overflowing gifts of God that are indeed more than enough for all. When we share in the bread of holy communion, with what we might call its ecological or economic proposal, we are certainly sharing in food. But we are also sharing in the land that produces such food. And in these very things, shared equitably in the name of God, we are, according to the scriptures proclaimed in worship, sharing in communion with each other and with God.

The prayer at the meal attempts to give some words to the mystery of God's goodness flowing and pouring through creation. It may be considered an example of what theologian Paul Santmire calls humanity's "contemplative dominion" over the natural world.[6] Human dominion is expressed most profoundly, Santmire suggests, in our ability to look out over *everything* and to contemplate it, to pause in wonder, and then to hold all the living earth and its creatures before God in prayer. This *pause* to pray before consuming (before communion and before all our meals) may be a sacred sign for us of the limits on our consumption to which scripture and ecological reality call us.

For reflection and discussion

1. What sorts of experiences do you have with gardening or working on a farm?
2. What is the best way for your congregation to connect the offering in worship to the hungry people in your community? To hungry communities across the world?
3. How might your congregation best choose and serve the bread and wine for communion?

4. What causes hunger in your community? Could a local social worker describe some of the struggles of hungry people in your area? What could change in the "ecology" of your community that could end hunger in your community?

5
Earth to Earth

Bodies as earth

One of the ecological critiques leveled against contemporary dominant cultures concerns anthropocentrism, the way in which cultures place humans at the center of concern and view the cosmos from a selfishly human perspective. A similar critique might be addressed to Christian worship. Worship is often pictured as only a gathering of *humans*, exclusive of other sorts of creatures. Even the object of our worship appears to be the human figure of Jesus or even sometimes some sort of representation of God, the invisible one, as a human—and often an older human male. Picture God reaching out to touch Adam on the ceiling of the Sistine Chapel: worship as an interaction between one human figure on earth and another in the sky.

Why, instead, couldn't worship look more like New York City's Cathedral of St. John the Divine on St. Francis Day for its blessing of the animals, when the great doors open and camels, chimpanzees, elephants, and eagles join in the procession, are reverenced and join their voices and bodies in the song of all creation? Or couldn't we find a way for worship to be every bit as grand and biodiverse as, say, the Boundary Waters of Minnesota and Canada, the lush Appalachian

Cove forests, the painted high desert of northern New Mexico? Of course, worship in such places and among such diverse creatures can indeed include the voices, concerns, and landscapes of these local places. Our prayers anyplace on Earth can include wild places and the diversity of species in our homeland and elsewhere. Worship, however, often appears to be a thoroughly human event—a bunch of humans getting together to communicate with a distant divine human. That is worth a real critique and a whole set of suggestions for ongoing reform. Much of this book has been intended as a contribution to such a project.

But in this chapter we stay a bit more resolutely with the human assembly gathered for worship, a group of more-or-less hairy animals gathered together. We begin by remembering Augustine's description of the human body as "the earth we carry," and remember that our human bodies gathered for worship are dust, earth, and to dust, earth we shall return. Each of us, in our bodies, is earth. We will all have earth sprinkled over us some day and go back to being indistinguishable from the stuff in gardens, prairies, and the forest floor.

The scriptures do not encourage us to think of ourselves as earth only when we return to dust in our *death*, but also when we consider the story of our *origins*: think of the story of Genesis 2, when God scoops up the dirt, forms it, makes it stand up, and then blows into it to make it live and walk around. Earth: standing, walking, breathing, singing. This is the creature that comes through the door to worship: earth filled with the breath of God.

Lutheran ethicist Larry Rasmussen writes about the futility of trying to free ourselves from the earthy identity of our bodies:

> We are *always* rooted in earth as earth creatures. There is no other possibility. We are utterly dependent on earth at every moment of our lives, for everything—air, water, food, materials, and energy. We are made of earth's materials, beings of dust and breath. We are part of earth's history and a fashioner of it.

> So the issue is not whether we can escape earth; we cannot. We
> live *in* earth *as* earth.[1]

We may think of our skin as a relatively impermeable boundary between outside (environment) and inside (self/body), but there are extremely porous boundaries between what we call our bodies and what we call earth—if the boundary really exists at all. The invisible molecules of Earth's atmosphere freely float in and out of our bloodstream, stabilizing our mind and our very existence with each breath. The hungers and thirsts we know in our bodies are drives for the very same earthly nutrients for which other plants and animals hunger and out of which we are all composed. The eagle diving for the salmon is driven by a force that even now drives humans to the same fish. Our bodies are home to many thousands of living creatures that help us digest our food, that keep our skin healthy, and without which we would quickly die. In fact, most of the living cells on and in our body do not even carry human DNA: approximately 90 percent of the total living cells we carry as "our" bodies belong to non-human living creatures that help to sustain the bodily ecology in which we live.

Our bodies are wondrously a living part of the earth. This connection sometimes turns ominous: springs, aquifers, and drinking water all over the world now flow with detectable levels of pharmaceuticals. What we thought we were putting into our own veins now flows through the veins of the earth. And in the place—perhaps more than any other—where we would naturally expect perfectly nurturing human food, breast milk, for our most fragile humans, there are now pesticides, PCBs, and dioxin showing up widely. (Though breast milk remains unquestionably the most healthy food for infants.) What we have put on the earth now flows through our bodies, even to our breastfed infants. When human bodies come to worship, the earth comes with us, in our veins, in our bones.

In fact, in Christian worship, much of the earth that is present in the worship space is the human assembly itself. Most likely, there is more water in the bodies of the congregation (we are about 60 percent water) than in the baptismal font; there is probably more dirt, earth, sitting in the pews than in any planters or pots that hold our little trees or flowers.

When humans gather for worship, even if it would be in a spaceship, even on Mars, the earth would be there because human bodies are there. Where there are human bodies, there is earth. One way of beginning a discussion of worship and ecology is to take up Ash Wednesday's counsel again and remember that we are ourselves earth and will return to earth. Our bodies, our peculiar plots of ground, are "the earth we carry" into worship. They are the earth that we *are*.

Jesus and human bodies

Jesus, an earthy human body, interacted with other earthy human bodies. On some levels this is quite familiar to us. But as a sort of refresher, we might list some of the people who literally came into contact with Jesus—those who are touched by Jesus or who touch Jesus during his lifetime. Such a list becomes something a litany:

- Jesus' mother, Mary, at his birth
- Simeon, waiting at the temple to see the Messiah, holding the infant Jesus in his arms
- A man with leprosy
- Peter's mother-in-law who was sick with a fever
- A woman suffering from hemorrhages for twelve years
- A girl who had died
- A few sick people in Nazareth
- Two blind men who follow Jesus from the road into a house, begging
- Peter, when he was sinking and terrified in the sea
- Many different people who were sick in Gennesaret
- Peter, James, and John when they were cowering in fear on the mountain of transfiguration
- Two blind men along the road near Jericho

- A deaf man near the Sea of Galilee
- A blind man in Bethsaida
- A young boy with violent seizures
- Young children who the disciples were attempting to keep away
- A dead body on a funeral bier, a man who had been the only son of a widow
- A "woman of the city who was a known sinner," while at table with the Pharisees
- The disciples' feet, washed by Jesus
- The kiss exchanged with Judas on the Mount of Olives
- The slave of the high priest whose ear one of the disciples had cut off
- The soldiers and military police who interrogate, torture and execute Jesus
- Joseph of Arimathea and Nicodemus, taking Jesus' body from the cross to the tomb
- Mary Magdalene, at the garden tomb
- Thomas, at Jesus' invitation, touching Jesus' hands and side

If we reflect on this list, we will notice that many of the bodies—the earth—that Jesus touches are earth that has been thrown out of balance, mistreated, abused, or is simply suffering for unknown reasons and is not whole, not flourishing. In Jesus' day, many of these bodies, this earth being carried, would have literally been called *polluted*—the lepers, the bleeding women, the sinners, feet, the sick, and the dead. Jesus' ministry with these bodies, these breathing plots of land, is to restore them to wholeness, to fruitfulness, to restore their relationships within and without, to cultivate what we might even call *ecological* flourishing.

This is part of a process that the New Testament calls "salvation." And when we picture the bodies named in this litany, it is easy to see the connection between the English word *salvation* and its Latin root *salvus*—which means health, wholeness, integrity, balance, safety. Jesus comes to restore deep *salvus* to these earthly bodies. When we toast someone one and say "salut!" we are drinking to their health. Here it is obvious that "salvation" means something much more complete and all-encompassing than our souls leaving our bodies and the earth behind to get to some unworldly heaven. Salvation as wholeness, as *health* in its deepest sense, is closely akin to what we might call "ecological integrity:" this body of earth being at peace with itself and in healthy relationship with the earth around it. We can see that process happening in the bodies named in the litany above.

This ministry of healing—bodies of earth praying for the healing of other bodies of earth—has been handed down to us today and is commended for use in our common worship and in other settings. The rites for healing in *Evangelical Lutheran Worship* recover some of the dignity and care shown to bodies in worship that had over centuries receded in liturgical practice, as if such practices (a large part of Jesus' and the apostles' ministry) were not spiritual enough, or were even dangerously distracting. Recovering the practices of healing prayer with anointing and laying on of hands is, on one level, simply a recovery of scripturally rooted liturgical practice commended by our ancestors in faith and by God's own action in Christ through the power of the Spirit. On another level, the practice is also consistent with an eco-theological movement that honors the created and earthly nature of our bodies and seeks to approach our bodies reverently as temples of the Holy Spirit.

Jesus and other ecological bodies

Theologian Sallie McFague writes about Jesus' ministry with human bodies and considers how this ministry corresponds to God's love and care for *other* bodies—bodies of water, bodies of land, forests, fields, and even planetary bodies. God creates, heals, and renews broken bodies, and even resurrects crucified bodies.

Thus, God's care for bodies is one powerful ecological connection to worship. However we might judge our congregations to be ready or not to engage in worship that is in an informed dialogue with the latest ecological science, most of our home congregations know how to pray for the healing of bodies. In congregations all over the world, Christians young and old know how to pray for and take care of those who are sick. *Worship* (with its prayers for healing and comfort) correlates closely with *action* (carrying food, taking care of relatives, visiting people in the hospital, helping people change a diet, quit smoking, or get out of an abusive relationship).

While we deepen our ministry with human bodies, perhaps we can also take the simple step of expanding our healing ministries (including prayer) outward to include local bodies of water, local landforms, forests, animals and entire species, mountains, air, and aquifers, using the images of healing that we know already from our communal prayer and from the scriptures. Some congregations already are becoming accustomed to praying for the health of local and distant ecological bodies, naming them aloud in their weekly intercessory prayers: the Gulf of Mexico, Puget Sound, a tall-grass prairie, a neighborhood threatened by toxic emissions, a small creek running near the church building, a mountain overlooking the town, or a nearby forest.

Most congregations can at least imagine a parish nurse program and many have one as a natural action-oriented outgrowth of their prayers for the sick. What sort of action-oriented practices might grow out of regular congregational prayer for the earth and its ecological bodies?

In short, our congregations largely know how to pray for and care for human bodies in a way that holds together prayer and action. That knowledge and practice now can expand outward to enfold other bodies. In this way, ecological piety and ecological action can profoundly enter our worship and our practice in a way that already feels largely familiar.

Dying in Christ, on Earth

Even those bodies healed by Jesus eventually died, as does all flesh. The event of death invites—even presses upon us—questions about the purpose of life and of creaturely existence. How are we to relate to those who die? What is our life actually *for*? Is death a return to the earth or an escape from the earth? Our worship at the time of death includes proclamation of the living Word of God that interprets our life and death itself in light of the good news of God in Jesus Christ. Part of that proclamation occurs in the preaching at a funeral. But that is not the only proclamation. The rituals themselves preach.

Over the past decades, a growing movement has increasingly questioned what is being "preached" in modern North American funeral practices, especially concerning reverence for the body, the goodness of the earth, and the basic reality of humans returning to dust, to earth, in death. This movement, sometimes called the Green Funeral or Green Burial movement, has adapted older and more traditional practices around death for use in our current ecological age. The overall concern of this movement is for our deaths to be, in biblical language, "dust to dust." More specifically, the varied practices of this diverse movement ritualize our deaths in ways that return us to the dust without the use of toxic embalming chemicals, without huge amounts of materials buried with us (for example, large and elaborate coffins and vaults), and without destroying the ecological integrity of our bodies or our resting places. Typically, all of these practices also allow for more opportunities for participation in the care of the body, for prayer and ritual, for honoring the body, and for resonance with scriptural texts. And these practices are often much less expensive than what has become the North American cultural norm.

Care of the body

Ecological care for the body just after the actual time of death has generally involved two sets of practices: those concerning the *location* of the body for the viewing or wake, and those concerning the *care* for the body itself before burial. First is the question of where the body of the deceased will rest after death and until the funeral. Many people are now familiar with the work of hospice, which, in addition to their work in hospitals and nursing homes, also provides support for people who wish to die at home rather than in a hospital or nursing home. In ways that are quite similar to hospice, many families are now working with trained caregivers who guide them through caring for the bodies of their loved ones, before, at, and after death, all while remaining at home. In an act recalling baptism and the care shown Jesus' body by his followers after his death, trained caregivers may help family members lovingly wash and clothe the body of the deceased, and prepare the body for viewing, funeral, and burial. A number of established organizations offer support and trained caregivers who guide families through this process, typically planning ahead with families during advanced age or terminal illness.[2]

An emerging practice in the green funeral movement is a home viewing, sometimes called a wake, and perhaps even a home funeral. This practice of gathering at the home of the deceased, after death, with family members keeping vigil and the body lying peacefully in a bed, was, of course, common until the relatively recent practice of renting another (funeral) home for such a gathering after death. As families have moved farther apart, the time required for long-distance travel has also led to the practice of keeping bodies for days at a funeral home, rather than keeping vigil with the body at home for a day or two, and then holding the funeral and burial. One result of this shift toward funeral homes has been for people to experience death as increasingly unnatural, something apart from the ecology of everyday life.

The place of the body at home after death may deepen our experience of the home as holy ground, as grieving, prayers, hymns, mutual consolation, vigil-keeping, silence, and storytelling may take place in the company of our loved one's body—in the place of daily life. The rites and prayers in the "Ministry at the Time of Death" section of *Evangelical Lutheran Worship Pastoral Care* are especially suited for this time. Deaths marked at home continue to be just as wrenching, painful, and even tragic as other deaths. Yet deaths marked at home, before the funeral itself, are also clearly marked out as a part of *life*. One of the most destructive and painful modern distortions of ecological reality is the exemption of human death from what is considered a natural part of earth's ecology, and even of human ecology. Not only does this distortion cause the event of death to seem all the more alien and frightening, but it also lessens the opportunities for regular honest reflection on mortality—reflections that may serve as a check on an anxious, shallow, ecologically destructive consumerism.

When bodies are cared for in the home, it is often the case that, before death, the deceased or the family has stated their wish to forego the modern processes of surgically invasive and chemically toxic embalming. Such practices were not widely practiced in North America until the transportation of bodies over long distances in the civil war began a tendency toward chemical embalming of all bodies. Formaldehyde-based embalming fluids are toxic and appear to be linked to cancer and other diseases, and may contribute to the high rate of leukemia observed among pathologists and embalmers. In many religions today the time-honored practices of caring for bodies—reverently washing them and preparing them for viewing and burial (instead of embalming them)—are ritually handed on to each new generation. It is often considered a great honor to participate in the care of the bodies of loved ones after death. In fact, many present-day Jews and Muslims consider modern surgical/chemical embalming practices to be a religious offense, the abuse of a corpse. However, growing numbers of even conventional funeral homes are now offering alternatives to toxic embalming chemicals, including cooling of the body in the days before burial, or the use of nontoxic embalming fluids. In all of these questions, planning ahead is important. The Green Burial Council offers an extensive database of advice, resources, and professional caregivers who can guide the planning and honor the wishes of the family.

Burial vessel

The top surface of the American cemetery is typically ten acres of green grass. But looking at what is below ground may blur the line between *burial ground* and *landfill*. The average American cemetery holds an enormous amount of landfilled material: enough coffin wood to build more than 40 houses, 1,000 tons of casket steel, and 20,000 tons of vault concrete.[3] Every year, U.S. cemeteries bury 30 million board feet of timber, 90,000 tons of steel, and 1.6 million tons of concrete for vaults.[4] This is a direct result of the peculiar patterns of our death rituals.

Modern coffins are often elaborate, heavy, ornate, and expensive. Some look like space capsules, possessing a literally extra-terrestrial appearance. Many are even marketed as being resistant to biodegradation, thus attempting to enclose our deaths in an anti-ecological lie. This is a relatively new phenomenon. Coffins in the United States, until the mid- to late-1800s, were typically made of unadorned wood in a simple hexagonal form, with a single flat lid. Many people, in fact, constructed their own coffins long before they reached significant illness or old age, keeping the coffin in a barn or a loft, sometimes even playfully napping in it, in preparation for their long sleep in the earth. In fact, the word *casket* only referred to a small, richly ornamented box for jewels or other precious possessions until the mid-nineteenth century, when coffin makers began selling much more elaborate burial vessels, now marketed as caskets.

Many people today are returning to simpler and more ecologically benign burial vessels, including simple wooden or basketlike coffins, and burial shrouds. Ecologically appropriate burial vessels are produced from biodegradable, natural, and sustainable materials.

One Christian community of Trappist monks works to support their life of prayer by building simple, beautiful coffins using the wood from the sustainably harvested forests on their land. For these monks of the New Melleray Abbey near Dubuque, Iowa, their life of prayer is closely integrated to their care for the land and for the dead. For each coffin that they make, the monks plant a tree—and pray a blessing for it. In their common worship, they pray by name for the families and loved ones of those who have died and for whom they have built a coffin.

Funeral directors are required by law to allow families to choose coffins purchased or built elsewhere, and the options for ecologically appropriate coffins, urns, and shrouds are now plentiful. Their cost can be significantly lower than highly manufactured coffins, and can cost in the hundreds of dollars or even be free (in the case of home-made coffins or blankets and quilts). These vessels are normally not placed in a vault but into an earthen grave. And in any case a funeral pall may best cover the burial vessel during the funeral—a sign of the deceased being still clothed in Christ as on their baptismal day.

Committal to the earth

When the dead are buried at Ramsey Creek Burial Grounds in South Carolina, the procession to the grave is accompanied not only by psalms and other scripture texts read by the minister. The sound of leaves underfoot, a pileated woodpecker in the forest canopy above, the sound of falling water in the creek, crickets, and tree frogs add their song to the woodland air. The funeral procession follows the open path through the woods to a grove in the forest chosen by the family where a simple grave has been dug. Pine needles cover the ground around the grave, and a large basket of wildflowers has been placed at its head. The rich, red, earth is piled up nearby. The funeral party is gathered around the grave. The presider leads the committal rite; certain prayers seem to resonate more deeply here, in a place so clearly a part of the cycles of death and life, and a grave so obviously of the earth. The pallbearers use leather or burlap straps to gently support the coffin as it is lowered into the grave. Members of the funeral party cast earth on the coffin while praying or speaking a blessing, and then some take turns filling the grave with earth using shovels provided by the staff of Ramsey Creek. The earth is mounded up over the grave, as it will settle over time. Some of the funeral party then, with their hands and some simple garden tools, open a few shallow spaces in the mounded earth and plant ferns, trees, and other native plants, watering them deeply, and then covering the remaining earth with pine needles from the forest floor. Finally, a large fieldstone that has been carved with a cross and the name and life span of the deceased is placed at the head of the grave. After a final prayer and blessing, the funeral party begins to leave, walking quietly down the path, or lingering together in groups in prayer and reflection.

Along with other protections for the nature preserve, the legal protections granted to this and other graves ensure that the land of Ramsey Creek will continue to be legally protected as a nature preserve, sheltering old growth forest, a pristine stream, and over 200 species of plants. Thus, as the bodies lie in rest in the earth, they also protect a place of flourishing life, perhaps, for Christians, a sign of the power of Christ's resurrection.

Many of the practices described in this chapter are in fact already commended in *Evangelical Lutheran Worship* and in many other Christian worship resources. These include a coffin carried in procession to the grave; the reading of scripture; the sprinkling or shoveling of earth over the coffin; language at the commendation that reflects the scriptural teaching of 'earth to earth, dust to dust;' and counsel to lower the coffin into the ground while the assembly is still gathered at the grave. This last practice allows the mourners the psychologically important witness that their loved one's body does indeed now rest in peace in the earth. Similar practices are adapted for families choosing cremation after death.

In all these emerging funeral practices (and for funeral planning in general), it is good to plan well in advance by studying scripture, reading through the funeral rites, talking with loved ones and ministers about preferences and hopes, making arrangements with service providers. Of course, in the end, death is a strong reminder that we are not in control of everything, and even the most careful planning can be frustrated by unforeseen events. In such cases, the promise that nothing in heaven or on earth can separate us from the love of God in Christ is all the more a vital part of the funeral proclamation. Exceptional circumstances, however, should not keep us from planning. Without planning, in our current cultures, many of these emerging practices are difficult to carry out. Planning ahead, in any case, may help us come to know all the more deeply, at the time of any death, that in our deaths we do indeed rest securely in Christ and in God's good earth.

Seeds dying in the ground bearing good fruit

The trends in green funeral practices both move away from recent ecologically problematic practices and move toward modern adaptation of older practices that are more in harmony with the natural, ecological rhythms of life and death. In the care of the body at the time of death, green funeral practices are moving away from expensive, rote, surgical, and chemically-toxic embalming carried out in a funeral center, and are instead moving toward prayerful, natural, simple, intentional, guided, and inexpensive care for the body in the home. With burial vessels, green funeral practices are moving away from burial in massive, expensive, ostensibly protective, landfilled, resource-intensive, sealed capsules, toward simple, inexpensive, sustainably produced, natural urns, coffins, or shrouds in which to return bodies to the earth. And with regard to the place of burial, green funeral practices are moving away from mown homogenous lawns with concrete vaults, with the actual burial hidden from the funeral party, toward simple, earth-nurturing, participative burial in an ecologically flourishing setting, often with the burial itself helping to protect the ecological integrity of the land.

The trends in green funeral practices are generally consistent with the hopes and reforms of ecumenical Christian funeral practices, offering more opportunities for participation in the care for the body and in prayer and ritual; more resonance in the funeral practices with scriptural images and texts; often less expense and less pressure toward consumerism; more intentionality about preparation, study, and discernment in funeral planning; a less anxious approach to death and embodiment; and a strong connection between the event of death and faith in God's healing and the power of Christ's resurrection.

A watered garden

Humans first came into existence in an already flourishing garden with towering forest canopies; deep thickets of leaves and fruits; great herds of animals thundering across the plains; rain, cascades, and streams watering the ground; flocks of birds that could blot out the sun; and over the majority of the surface of the earth, oceans swarming with creatures from the crests of waves to the darkest depths. The scriptures attest that this watered garden of the earth has been at worship since the beginning: the morning stars sang together and shouted for joy (Job 38:7), creatures look to God to give them their food in due season (Ps. 104:27), mountains and hills burst into song, and all the trees of the field clap their hands (Isa. 55:12). Amid this great diversity, humans also worship God. Christians have joined the earth's great liturgy, led into worship by Jesus Christ, whom we know as the firstborn of the new creation.

Our contemporary situation is not simple. We live in an age of ecological emergency, a crisis more pressing than any other that humanity has faced in the past. It is something new even for the earth itself: never before has a single species so profoundly disrupted the health of earth's life-support systems and other species. On our exodus out of bondage to our current patterns of ecological destruction, God will certainly lead us "by paths as yet untrodden, through perils unknown" (*Evangelical Lutheran Worship*, 304). We will need to find unprecedented and inventive ways of responding to this emergency. And yet in the new challenges of this age the world deeply needs a people who faithfully carry with them the ancient, sacred memory of God's gift of a good, living earth—a creature made by God that has a life of its own, that lives and can die, that is being healed even now by the power of the Spirit, and that is deeply beloved by its maker who suffers bodily with and in the earth. This memory, this Word, was in the beginning with God and is the living word that animates Christian worship today. Into our bodies of earth assembled for worship, the ancient Word that is the alpha and the omega, the beginning and the end, speaks to us in our age of ecological emergency: "See, I am making all things new. To the thirsty I will give water as a gift from the spring of the water of life" (Rev. 21:5-6). That word is *challenge* to us—a command for us to change our ways—and a *promise* that God faithfully gives renewal and new life, flowing like a spring of living water to the garden of the whole earth.

For reflection and discussion

1. What do you think of praying for nonhuman creatures in the prayers of intercession in worship?
2. What parts of the human and nonhuman creation do you think are especially in need of healing—locally, regionally, globally?
3. Do you normally think of your body as part of the earth? How or how not?
4. What sort of land and what sort of burial vessel do you prefer for your own burial?
5. Does your congregation (corporately or as individuals) carry out actions that seek to heal the earth's ecology toward flourishing, abundant life? Do you pray as a congregation for the places for which you work for healing?
6. Are there local green funeral service providers in your community? What services do they offer?

Notes

Chapter 1

1. For a wise account of the question of the orientation to the cosmos in worship, including the question of "up," see Gordon Lathrop's *Holy Ground: A Liturgical Cosmology* (Fortress Press, 2003).

2. In any case, in the very far-off future, there seems to be little question about the mortality of planet Earth or any other planet or star: all planets and stars have natural life cycles. Scientists predict that Earth will die of natural causes—being consumed by our sun—sometime around eight billion years from now.

3. "Abandon Earth—Or Face Extinction," interview with Stephen Hawking, *Big Think,* 2010, http://bigthink.com/ideas/21691 (accessed September 2010).

Chapter 2

1. Psalm 104:3, 10-17, 24. Translation composite.

2. *Didache,* 7:1-3.

3. Gordon Lathrop, *Holy Things: A Liturgical Theology* (Fortress Press, 1993), 94.

4. For this translation of the prayer see Frank C. Senn, *Christian Liturgy: Catholic and Evangelical* (Fortress Press, 1997), 289.

5. Large Catechism. Robert Kolb and Timothy J. Wengert, eds., *The Book of Concord* (Fortress Press, 2000), 461.

Chapter 3

1. A brief section of this chapter appears in revised form from "O Blessed Spring: Paschal Initiation in an Age of Ecological Disintegration." *Seattle University Theology Review* 6 (2006): 76–88.

2. Barbara Kingsolver, *The Poisonwood Bible* (New York: Flamingo-Harper, 1998), 45.

3. See three liturgical scholars from the southern hemisphere on these themes: Anscar Chupungco, *Shaping the Easter Feast* (Washington, D.C.: Pastoral Press, 1992); Clare V. Johnson, "Inculturating the Easter Feast in Southeast Australia," *Worship* 78, no. 2 (2004); and Carmel Pilcher, "Poinsettia: Christmas or Pentecost—Celebrating Liturgy in the Great South Land That Is Australia," *Worship* 81, no. 6 (2007).

4. Ambrose of Milan, "The Symbolism of the Approach to the Altar," in Edward Yarnold, ed., *The Awe-Inspiring Rites of Initiation: The Origins of the R.C.I.A*, 2nd ed. (Collegeville, Minn.: Liturgical Press, 1994), 128.

5. Cyril of Alexandria, Festal Letter IX; quoted in Anscar Chupungco, *Shaping the Easter Feast* (Washington, D.C.: Pastoral Press, 1992), 35.

6. Pseudo-Chrysostom, "A Complex Mystery," 7.3, in *Cantalemessa, Easter in the Early Church* (Collegeville, Minn.: Liturgical Press, 1993), 78.

Chapter 4

1. Some sections in this chapter appear in a revised form from their original publication in Benjamin Stewart, "Liturgical Preparation: Reviving the Center by Reaching Toward the Horizon," *Liturgical Ministry* 16 (Winter 2007): 30–35.

2. Gordon W. Lathrop, *Holy Ground: A Liturgical Cosmology* (Fortress Press, 2009), 150.

3. Chrissy Post and Callista Brown, "A Foretaste of the Feast to Come," *Holden Village News* 41 (Winter 2002): 14.

4. Mary Jo Leddy, *Radical Gratitude* (Maryknoll, N.Y.: Orbis, 2002), 52–53.

5. Leddy, *Radical Gratitude*, 63–64.

6. H. Paul Santmire, *The Travail of Nature: The Ambiguous Ecological Promise of Christian Theology* (Fortress Press, 1985), 69–70.

Chapter 5

1. Larry Rasmussen, *Earth Community, Earth Ethics* (Maryknoll, N.Y.: Orbis, 1996), 275–276.

2. Two of the most prominent networks offering these services are Crossings and Natural Transitions. See http://www.crossings.net and http://www.naturaltransitions.org.

3. John Berman and Joel Siegel, "Green Graveyards Offer Burial Without a Trace," *ABC News*, December 7, 2008, http://abcnews .go.com/Technology/GlobalWarming/story?id=6412762 (accessed September 6, 2010).

4. "Greening the Trip to the Great Beyond," *New York Times,* March 19, 2009, http://green.blogs.nytimes.com/2009/03/19/greening-the -trip-to-the-great-beyond/ (accessed September 6, 2010).

Bibliography

Brown, William P. *Seeing the Psalms: A Theology of Metaphor,* 1st ed. Louisville: Westminster John Knox, 2002.

Chupungco, Anscar J. *Shaping the Easter Feast.* NPM Studies in Church Music and Liturgy. Washington, D.C.: Pastoral Press, 1992.

Harris, Mark. *Grave Matters: A Journey through the Modern Funeral Industry to a Natural Way of Burial.* New York: Scribner, 2007.

Irwin, Kevin W. "The Sacramentality of Creation and the Role of Creation in Liturgy and Sacraments." In *Preserving the Creation: Environmental Theology and Ethics,* edited by Kevin W. Irwin and Edmund D. Pellegrino. Washington, D.C.: Georgetown University Press, 1994.

Johnson, Clare V. "Inculturating the Easter Feast in Southeast Australia." *Worship* 78, no. 2 (2004): 98-119.

Lathrop, Gordon. *Holy Ground: A Liturgical Cosmology.* Minneapolis: Fortress Press, 2003.

Louv, Richard. *Last Child in the Woods: Saving Our Children from Nature-Deficit Disorder.* Chapel Hill, N.C.: Algonquin, 2005.

Mick, Lawrence. *Liturgy and Ecology in Dialogue.* Collegeville, Minn.: Liturgical Press, 1997.

Ramshaw, Gail. Chapters on water and food in *Treasures Old and New: Images in the Lectionary*. Minneapolis: Fortress Press, 2002.

Santmire, H. Paul. *Ritualizing Nature: Renewing Christian Liturgy in a Time of Crisis*. Theology and the Sciences. Minneapolis: Fortress Press, 2008.

Stewart, Benjamin. "Flooding the Landscape: Luther's Flood Prayer and Baptismal Theology." *CrossAccent* 13, no. 1 (2005): 4-14.

"Surf Your Watershed." United States Environmental Protection Agency, http://cfpub.epa.gov/surf/locate/index.cfm (accessed April 2011).

"The Columbia River Watershed: Caring for Creation and the Common Good." *An International Pastoral Letter by the Catholic Bishops of the Region*, http://www.columbiariver.org/ (accessed April 2011).

Yarnold, Edward. *The Awe-Inspiring Rites of Initiation: The Origins of the R.C.I.A.*, 2nd ed. Collegeville, Minn.: Liturgical Press, 1994.

Titles in the Worship Matters Series

Why Worship Matters
Robert A. Rimbo; foreword by Mark S. Hanson
9780806651088
The first volume in the series. Written in the style of good preaching, this collection of bite-size essays is a conversation-starter for those who want to look at the assembly's worship in very broad terms.

A Christian Funeral: Witness to the Resurrection
Melinda A. Quivik
9780806651484
A theologically informed, pastorally astute, and ecumenically relevant guide to Christian funeral rites. Quivik helps the reader explore the deeper meaning of the Christian funeral so that the resources of private businesses in the burial event can be put to their proper use.

A Moving Word: Media Art in Worship
Eileen D. Crowley
9780806652863
Through examples of ways to integrate media art within worship services throughout the liturgical year, Crowley stretches readers' imaginations to envision a new kind of art—*liturgical media art*—and to take a new approach in producing it: *communal co-creation*.

A Place of Encounter: Renewing Worship Spaces
D. Foy Christopherson
9780806651071
In its 2000-year history the church has tried on many buildings, and is ever seeking a more comfortable skin. Exactly what that skin will look like is guided by how the church understands itself, by how it worships, and by what it understands its mission to be.

A Three-Year Banquet: The Lectionary for the Assembly
Gail Ramshaw
9780806651057
A concise, clear, straightforward introduction to the way that Christian communities have organized their reading of scripture in worship.

Central Things: Worship in Word and Sacrament
Gordon W. Lathrop
9780806651637
A revised and expanded edition of the 1994 classic *What are the essentials of Christian worship?*

Centripetal Worship: The Evangelical Heart of Lutheran Worship
Timothy J. Wengert, editor; with contributions from Mark Mummert, Melinda Quivik, Dirk G. Lange, and foreword by F. Russell Mitman
9780806670171
Examines how worship is, and should be, at the center of the assembly. Contributors look at the historical and contemporary factors that influence how and why we worship the way we do.

Daily Bread, Holy Meal: Opening the Gifts of Holy Communion
Samuel Torvend
9780806651064
Drawing on recent biblical and historical studies, this exploration of the eucharist asks the seeker in every Christian to consider the ecological, theological, communal, and ethical dimensions of the Lord's supper.

Flowing Water, Uncommon Birth:
Christian Baptism in a Post-Christian Culture
Samuel Torvend
9780806670638
Explore a rich, ancient, multifaceted, deeply Christian baptismal practice and theology. This book invites us to ask important questions about the central mystery of Holy Baptism and the fullness of the baptized life.

The Three-Day Feast: Maundy Thursday, Good Friday, Easter
Gail Ramshaw
9780806651156
Recent decades have witnessed the revival of the ancient liturgies of the Three Days—Maundy Thursday, Good Friday, and the Easter Vigil. In this book Ramshaw gives a little history and a lot of suggestions about how these services can enrich the worship life of your entire assembly.

Truly Present: Practicing Prayer in the Liturgy
Lisa E. Dahill
9780806651477
Dahill connects the liturgy to a series of spiritual practices that carry Sunday worship into the rest of the week. Each chapter is rooted in a central element of worship and is intended to help you engage that dimension of worship more fully and attentively.

What Song Shall We Sing?
John Ylvisaker
9780806651491
The noted writer and leader of assembly song explains how musical fusion can work in our congregations as they strive to make it through the thicket of the musical scene in today's churches.